THEOSOPHY

An Introduction to the Supersensible
Knowledge of the World and the
Destination of Man

THEOSOPHY

An Introduction to the Supersensible Knowledge of the World and the Destination of Man

by
RUDOLF STEINER

ANTHROPOSOPHIC PRESS, INC.
NEW YORK

This volume is a translation of *Theosophie, Einführung in übersinnliche Welterkenntnis und Menschenbestimmung* (Vol. 9 in the Bibliographic Survey, 1961). Translated by Henry B. Monges and revised for this edition by Gilbert Church, Ph.D.

This translation has been authorized for the Western Hemisphere by the Rudolf Steiner Nachlassverwaltung, Dornach, Switzerland.

Printed in the United States of America

Contents

FROM THE PREFACES TO THE FIRST, SECOND, AND THIRD EDITIONS

THE purpose of this book is to give a description of some of the regions of the supersensible world. The reader who is only willing to admit the existence of the sensible world will look upon this description as merely an unreal production of the imagination. Whoever looks for paths that lead beyond this world of the senses, however, will soon learn to understand that human life only gains in worth and significance through insight into another world. He will not, as many fear, be estranged from the "real" world through this new power of vision because only through it does he learn to stand securely and firmly in this life and learns to know the causes of life. Without this power of vision he gropes like a blind man through their effects. Only through the understanding of the supersensible does the sensible "real" acquire meaning. A man therefore becomes more and not less fit for life through this understanding. Only he who understands life can become a truly practical man.

The author of this book describes nothing to which he cannot bear witness from experience—the kind of experience that belongs to these regions. Nothing will be described here that has not been personally experienced in this sense.

This book cannot be read in the customary manner of the present day. In certain respects every page, and even many sentences, will have to be worked out by the reader. This has been aimed at intentionally because only in this way can the book become to the reader what it ought to be. The one who merely reads it through will not have read it at all. Its truths must be experienced, lived. Only in this sense has spiritual science any value.

The book cannot be judged from the standpoint of science if the point of view adopted in forming such a judgment is not gained from the book itself. If the critic will adopt this point of view, he will certainly see that the presentation of the facts given in this book will in no way conflict with truly scientific methods. The author is satisfied that he has taken care not to come into conflict with his own scientific scrupulousness even by a single word.

Those who feel more drawn to another method of searching after the truths here set forth will find such a method in my *Philosophy of Freedom*. The lines of thought taken in these two books, though different, lead to the same goal. For the understanding of the one, the other is by no means necessary, although undoubtedly helpful to some persons.

Those who look for "ultimate" truths in this book will perhaps lay it aside unsatisfied. The primary intention of the author has been to present the fundamental truths underlying the whole domain of spiritual science. It lies in the very nature of man to ask at once about the beginning and the end of the world, the purpose of existence, and the nature and being of God. Anyone, however, who looks not for mere phrases and concepts of the intellect, but for a real understanding of life, knows that in a work that deals with the elements of spiritual knowledge, things may not be said that belong to the higher stages of wisdom. It is indeed only through an understanding of these elements that it becomes clear how higher questions should be asked. In another work forming a continuation of this one, namely, in the author's *Occult Science, an Outline,* further particulars will be found on the subject here dealt with.

In the preface to a second edition of this book the following supplementary remarks were inserted: Anyone who at the present time gives a description of supersensible facts ought to be quite clear on two points. The first is that the cultivation of supersensible knowledge is a necessity for our age; the other is that the intellectual and spiritual life of the day is full of ideas and feelings that make a description like this appear to many as an absolute chaos of fantastic notions and dreams. Knowledge of the supersensible is a necessity today because all that a man can learn through current methods about the world and life arouses in him numerous questions. Those can be answered only by means of supersensible truths. We ought not to deceive ourselves with regard to the fact that the teaching concerning the fundamental truths of existence given within the intellectual and spiritual currents of today is for the deeply feeling soul a source, not of answers, but of questions about the great problems of the universe and of life. Some people may for a time hold firmly to the opinion that they can find a solution of the problems of existence within conclusions from strictly scientific facts, and within the deductions of this or that thinker of the day. But when the soul descends into those depths into which it must descend if it is to understand itself, what at first seemed to be an answer appears only as the incentive to the real question. An answer to this question does not merely have to satisfy human curiosity. On it depend the inner calm and completeness of the soul life. The attainment of such an answer does not satisfy merely the thirst for knowledge. It makes a man capable of practical work and fits him for the duties of life, while the lack of an answer to these questions lames his soul and finally his body also. In fact, the knowledge of the supersensible is not merely something that meets a theoretical requirement. It supplies a method for leading a truly practical life. It is just because of the nature of our present day intellectual life that study in the domain of spiritual knowledge is indispensable.

On the other hand it is an evident fact that many today reject most strongly what they most sorely need. Some people are so greatly influenced by theories built up on the basis of exact scientific experience that they cannot do otherwise than regard the contents of a book like this as a boundless absurdity. The exponent of supersensible truths is able to view such a fact entirely free from any illusions. People will certainly be prone to demand that he give irrefutable proofs for what he states, but they do not realize that in so doing they are the victims of a misconception. They demand, although unconsciously, not the proofs lying within the things themselves, but those that they personally are willing to recognize or are in a condition to recognize. The author of this book is sure that any person, taking his stand on the basis of the science of the present day, will find that it contains nothing that he will be unable to accept. He knows that all the requirements of modern science can be complied with, and for this very reason the method adopted here of presenting the facts of the supersensible world supplies its own justification. In fact, the way in which true modern science approaches and deals with a subject is precisely the one that is in full harmony with this presentation. Anyone who thinks thus will feel moved by many a discussion in a way described by Goethe's deeply true saying, "A false teaching does not offer any opening to refutation because it rests upon the conviction that the false is true." Argument is fruitless with those who allow only such proofs to weigh with them as fit in with their own way of thinking. Those who know the true nature of what is called "proving" a matter see clearly that the human soul finds truth through other means than by argument. It is with these thoughts in mind that the author offers this book for publication.

PREFACE TO THE
REVISED ENGLISH EDITION

THIS book has been carefully and thoroughly revised by me for each new edition. The substance of the first edition remains, it is true, unaltered, but in certain parts I have sought to bring the mode of expression more into accord with the content of spiritual vision. I have especially endeavored to do this in the chapter on *Re-Embodiment of the Spirit and Destiny* (*Karma*).

Descriptions of the supersensible must be treated differently from descriptions of the sensible world. They appeal to the reader in a different way. They demand more from him and he must work with the author more intensely in thought while reading. The author needs his co-operation to a far higher degree than does one who writes descriptions drawn from the regions of the sensory world. Many critics will perhaps complain because I have made special efforts to comply with this demand in my description of the spiritual world. The spiritual world, however, has not the definite outlines of the physical, and if anyone were to represent it so as to give the impression that this was the case, he would be describing something untrue. In describing the spiritual world of facts, the style must be in accordance with the mobile, flowing character of that world.

Inner truth for descriptions of the spiritual world belongs alone to what is expressed in flowing, mobile ideas. The peculiar character of the spiritual world must be carried over into the ideas. If the reader applies the standard to which he is accustomed from descriptions of the sensory world, he will find it difficult to adapt himself to this different method of description.

It is by inner exertion of soul that the human being is able to reach the supersensible world. That world would, indeed, have no value if it lay spread out wholly before his consciousness. It would then be in no way different from the sensuous world. Before it can be known, the longing must be present to find what lies more deeply hidden in existence than do the forces of the world perceived by the senses. This longing is one of the inner experiences that prepare the way for a knowledge of the supersensible world. Even as there can be no blossom without first the root, so supersensible knowledge has no true life without this longing.

It would, however, be a mistake to suppose that the ideas of the supersensible world arise as an illusion of this longing. The lungs do not create the air for which they long, neither does the human soul create out of its longing the ideas of the supersensible world. The soul has this longing because it is formed and built for the supersensible world, just as the lungs are constructed for the air.

There may be those who say that this supersensible world can only have significance for such as already have the power to perceive it, but this is not so. There is no need to be a painter in order to feel the beauty of a painting, yet only a painter can paint it. In the same sense it is unnecessary to be a researcher in the supersensible in order to judge the truth of the results of supersensible research. It is only necessary to be a researcher in order to discover them. This is right in principle. In the last chapter of this book, however—and in detail in others of my books—the methods are given whereby it is possible for anyone to become a researcher in the supersensible world, and thus be in a position to test the results of such research.

Rudolf Steiner

April, 1922

INTRODUCTION

WHEN in the autumn of 1813, Johann Gottlieb Fichte gave to the world as the ripe fruit of a life wholly devoted to the service of truth, his *Introduction to the Science of Knowledge,* he said at the very outset, "This doctrine presupposes an entirely new inner sense organ or instrument through which a new world is revealed having no existence for the ordinary man." He then showed by a simile how incomprehensible this doctrine must be when judged by conceptions of the ordinary senses. "Think of a world of people born blind who, therefore, know only those objects and relations that exist through the sense of touch. Go among them, and speak to them of colors and the other relations that exist only through light and for the sense of sight. You will convey nothing to their minds, and this will be the more fortunate if they tell you so, for you will then quickly notice your mistake and, if unable to open their eyes, you will cease talking in vain . . ."

Now those who speak about such things as Fichte does in this instance, often find themselves in the position of a normal man among those born blind. Yet these are things that relate to a man's true being and highest goal, and to believe it necessary "to cease talking in vain" would be to despair of humanity. We ought not to doubt for one moment the possibility of opening the eyes of every earnest person to these things. On this supposition all those have written and spoken who have felt within themselves that the inner sense-instrument had developed, thereby enabling them to know the true nature and being of man, which is generally hidden from the outer senses. Hence from the most ancient times such a *hidden wisdom* has been spoken of again and again. Those who have grasped some under-standing of it feel just as sure of their possession as people with normal eyes feel sure of their ability to visualize color. For them this hidden wisdom requires no proof. They know also that this hidden wisdom requires no proof for anyone else to whom the "higher sense" has unfolded itself. They can speak to such a person as a traveler can speak about America to people who have themselves never seen that country but who can visualize it, for they would see all that he has seen were the opportunity to present itself to them.

It is not, however, only to researchers into the spiritual world that the observer of the supersensible has to speak. He must address his words to all men, because he has to give an account of things that concern all men. Indeed, he knows that without a knowledge of these things no one can, in the true sense of the word, be a human being. Thus, he speaks to all men because he knows there are different degrees of understanding for what he has to say. The

xviii

feeling for truth and the power of understanding it are inherent in everyone, and he knows that even those who are still far from the moment in which they will acquire the ability to make their own spiritual research can bring a measure of understanding to meet him. He addresses himself first to this understanding that can flash forth in every healthy soul. He knows that in this understanding there is a force that must slowly lead to the higher degrees of knowledge. This feeling, which perhaps at first perceives nothing at all of what it is told, is itself the magician that opens the "eye of the spirit." In darkness this feeling stirs. The soul sees nothing, but through this feeling it is seized by the power of truth. The truth then gradually draws nearer to the soul and opens the higher sense in it. In one person it may take a longer, in another a shorter time. Everyone, however, who has patience and endurance reaches this goal, for although not every physical eye can be operated on, every spiritual eye can be opened. When it will be opened is only a question of time.

Erudition and scientific training are not prerequisite conditions for the unfolding of this higher sense. It can develop in the unsophisticated person just as in the renowned scientist. Indeed, what is often called at the present time the only true science can, for the attainment of this goal, be frequently a hindrance rather than a help because this science considers real only what is accessible to the ordinary senses. Its merits in regard to the knowledge of that reality may be ever so great, yet when science declares that what is necessary and a blessing for itself shall also be authoritative for all human knowledge, it thereby creates a mass of prejudices that close the approach to higher realities.

The objection is often made to what has just been said that insurmountable limits have been once and forever set to man's knowledge, and since a man cannot overstep these limits, all knowledge must be rejected that does not take them into account. Furthermore, the one who presumes to make assertions about things, which for many stand proved as lying beyond the limits of man's capacity for knowledge, is looked upon as being highly immodest. In making such objections the fact is entirely disregarded that a development of the human powers of knowledge must precede the higher knowledge. What lies beyond the limits of knowledge before such a development takes place is, after the awakening of faculties slumbering in every man, entirely within the realm of knowledge.

One point in this connection must not be neglected. It might be said, "Of what use is it to speak to people about things for which their powers of knowledge are not yet awakened and are therefore still closed to them?" This is really the wrong way to view the matter. Certain powers are required to discover the things referred to, but if after having been discovered they are made known, every person can understand them who is willing to bring to them unprejudiced logic and a healthy sense of truth. In this book the things made known are wholly of a kind that must produce the impression that through them the riddles of human life and the phenomena of the world can be satisfactorily approached. This impression will be produced upon everyone who permits thought, unclouded by prejudice, and a feeling for truth, free and without reservation, to work within him. Put yourself for a moment in the position of asking, "If the things asserted here are true, do they afford a satisfying explanation of life?" You will find that the life of every man supplies a confirmation.

In order to be a teacher in these higher regions of existence it is by no means sufficient to have simply developed the sense for them. To that end science is just as necessary as it is for the teacher's calling in the world of ordinary reality. Higher seeing alone does not make a knower in the spiritual any more than healthy sense organs make a scholar in the realm of sensible realities. Because in truth all reality, the lower as well as the higher spiritual, are only two sides of one and the same fundamental being, anyone who is ignorant in the lower branches of knowledge will as a rule remain ignorant in the higher. This fact creates a feeling of immeasurable responsibility in the person who, through a spiritual call, feels himself summoned to speak about the spiritual regions of existence. It imposes upon him humility and reserve. This should deter no one —not even those whose other circumstances of life afford them no opportunity for the study of ordinary science— from occupying himself with the higher truths. Everyone can fulfill his task as a man without understanding anything of botany, zoology, mathematics and the other sciences. He cannot, however, in the full sense of the word, be a human being without having come in some way or other nearer to an understanding of the nature and destination of man as revealed through the knowledge of the super-sensible.

The highest to which a man is able to look, he calls the Divine, and he somehow must think of the highest destiny as being in connection with this Divinity. The wisdom, therefore, that reaches out beyond the sensible and reveals to him his own being and with it his final goal, may well be called *divine wisdom* or *theosophy*. To the study of the spiritual processes in human life and in the cosmos, the term *spiritual science* may be given. When, as in this book, one extracts from this spiritual science those special results that have reference to the spiritual core of man's being, then the expression *theosophy* may be employed to designate this domain because it has been employed for centuries in this way.

From this point of view there will be sketched in this book an outline of the theosophical conception of the universe. The writer of it will bring forward nothing that is not a fact for him in the same sense that an experience of the outer world is a fact for eyes and ears and the ordinary intelligence. The concern here is with experiences that become accessible to everyone who is determined to tread the path of knowledge described in a later chapter of this book. We take the right attitude towards the things of the supersensible world when we assume that sound thinking and feeling are capable of understanding everything of true knowledge that emerges from the higher worlds. Further, when we start from this understanding and therewith lay down a firm foundation, we have also made a great step forward towards "seeing" for ourselves, even though in order to attain this, other things must be added also. We lock and bolt the door to the true higher knowledge, however, when we despise this road and are determined to penetrate the higher worlds only in some other way. To have decided to recognize higher worlds only when we have seen them is a hindrance in the way of this very seeing itself. The determination to understand first through sound thinking what later can be seen, furthers that seeing. It conjures forth important powers of the soul that lead to this seeing of the seer.

THEOSOPHY

An Introduction to the Supersensible
Knowledge of the World and the
Destination of Man

CHAPTER I

THE ESSENTIAL NATURE OF MAN

THE following words of Goethe point beautifully to the beginning of one way by which the essential nature of man can be known. "As soon as a person becomes aware of the objects around him, he considers them in relation to himself, and rightly so, because his whole fate depends on whether they please or displease him, attract or repel, help or harm him. This quite natural way of looking at or judging things appears to be as easy as it is necessary. A person is, nevertheless, exposed through it to a thousand errors that often make him ashamed and embitter his life.

"A far more difficult task is undertaken by those whose keen desire for knowledge urges them to strive to observe the objects of nature as such and in their relationship to each other. These individuals soon feel the lack of the test that helped them when they, as men, regarded the objects in reference to themselves personally. They lack the test of pleasure and displeasure, attraction and repulsion, usefulness and harmfulness. Yet this test must be renounced entirely. They ought as dispassionate and, so to speak, divine beings, to seek and examine what is, not what gratifies. Thus the true botanist should not be moved either by the beauty or by the usefulness of the plants. He must study their formation and their relation to the rest of the plant kingdom. They are one and all enticed forth and shone upon by the sun without distinction, and so he should, equably and quietly, look at and survey them all and obtain the test for this knowledge, the data for his deductions, not out of himself, but from within the circle of the things he observes."

This thought thus expressed by Goethe directs man's attention to three divisions of things. First, the objects concerning which information continually flows to him through the doors of his senses—the objects he touches, smells, tastes, hears and sees. Second, the impressions that these make on him, characterizing themselves through the fact that he finds the one sympathetic, the other abhorrent, the one useful, another harmful. Third, the knowledge that he, as a "so to speak divine being," acquires concerning the objects, that is, the secrets of their activities and their being as they unveil themselves to him.

These three divisions are distinctly separate in human life, and man thereby becomes aware that he is interwoven with the world in a threefold way. The first division is one that he finds present, that he accepts as a given fact. Through the second he makes the world into his own affair, into something that has a meaning for

2

him. The third he regards as a goal towards which he ought unceasingly to strive.

Why does the world appear to man in this threefold way? A simple consideration will explain it. I cross a meadow covered with flowers. The flowers make their colors known to me through my eyes. That is the fact I accept as given. Having accepted the fact, I rejoice in the splendor of the colors. Through this I turn the fact into an affair of my own. Through my feelings I connect the flowers with my own existence. Then, a year later I go again over the same meadow. Other flowers are there. Through them new joy arises in me. My joy of the former year will appear as a memory. This is in me. The object that aroused it in me is gone, but the flowers I now see are of the same kind as those I saw the year before. They have grown in accordance with the same laws as have the others. If I have informed myself regarding this species and these laws, I then find them again in the flowers of this year, just as I found them in those of last year. So I shall perhaps muse, "The flowers of last year are gone and my joy in them remains only in my memory. It is bound up with my existence alone. What I recognized in the flowers of last year and recognize again this year, however, will remain as long as such flowers grow. That is something that revealed itself to me, but it is not dependent on my existence in the same way as my joy is. My feelings of joy remain in me. The laws, the being of the flowers, remain outside of me in the world."

3

By these means man continually links himself in this threefold way with the things of the world. One should not, for the present, read anything into this fact, but merely take it as it stands. From this it can be seen that man has three sides to his nature. This and nothing else will, for the present, be indicated here by the three words, *body, soul* and *spirit*. Whoever connects any preconceived opinions or even hypotheses with these three words will necessarily misunderstand the following explanations. By *body* is here meant that through which the things in the environment of a man reveal themselves to him, as in the above example, the flowers in the meadow. By the word *soul* is signified that by which he links the things to his own being, through which he experiences pleasure and displeasure, desire and aversion, joy and sorrow in connection with them. By *spirit* is meant what becomes manifest in him when, as Goethe expressed it, he looks at things as a "so to speak divine being." In this sense man consists of *body, soul* and *spirit*.

Through his body man is able to place himself for the time being in connection with things; through his soul he retains in himself the impressions they make on him; through his spirit there reveals itself to him what the things retain for themselves. Only when we observe man in these three aspects can we hope to throw light on his whole being, because they show him to be related in a threefold way to the rest of the world.

Through his body man is related to the objects that

4

present themselves to his senses from without. The materials from the outer world compose his body, and the forces of the outer world work also in it. He observes the things of the outer world with his senses, and he also is able to observe his own bodily existence. It is impossible, however, for him to observe his soul existence in the same way. Everything in him that is bodily process can be perceived with his bodily senses. His likes and dislikes, his joy and pain, neither he nor anyone else can perceive with bodily senses. The region of the soul is inaccessible to bodily perception. The bodily existence of a man is manifest to all eyes; the soul existence he carries within himself as his world. Through the spirit, however, the outer world is revealed to him in a higher way. The mysteries of the outer world, indeed, unveil themselves in his inner being. He steps in spirit out of himself and lets the things speak about themselves, about what has significance not for him but for them. For example, man looks up at the starry heavens. The delight his soul experiences belongs to him. The eternal laws of the stars that he comprehends in thought, in spirit, belong not to him but to the stars themselves.

In this way, man is a citizen of three worlds. Through his *body* he belongs to the world that he also perceives through his body; through his *soul* he constructs for himself his own world; through his *spirit* a world reveals itself to him that is exalted above both the others.

It seems obvious that because of the essential differ-

5

ences of these three worlds, a clear understanding of them
and of man's share in them can only be obtained by means
of three different modes of observation.

1. The Corporeal Nature of Man

We learn to know man's body through bodily senses,
and the manner of observing it cannot differ from the way
in which we learn to know other objects perceived by the
senses. As we observe minerals, plants and animals, so
can we also observe man. He is related to these three forms
of existence. Like the minerals, he builds his body out of
natural substances; like the plants, he grows and propagates his species; like the animals, he perceives the objects
around him and builds up his inner experiences on the
basis of the impressions they make on him. Thus, a mineral, a plant and an animal existence may be ascribed to
man.

The differences in structure of minerals, plants and
animals correspond with the three forms of their existence. It is this structure—the shape—that is perceived
through the senses, and that alone can be called body.
Now the human body is different from that of the animal.
This difference must be recognized, whatever may otherwise be thought of the relationship of man to animals.
Even the most extreme materialist who denies all soul
cannot but admit the truth of this passage uttered by
Carus in his *Organon der Natur und des Geistes*. "The

finer, inner construction of the nervous system and especially of the brain remains still an unsolved problem for the physiologist and the anatomist. That this concentration of structures ever increases in the animal kingdom and reaches in man a stage unequalled in any other being is a fully established fact—a fact that is of the deepest significance in regard to the mental evolution of man. Indeed, we may go so far as to say it is really a sufficient explanation of that evolution. Where, therefore, the structure of the brain has not developed properly, where its smallness and poverty are in evidence as in the case of microcephali and idiots, it goes without saying that we can no more expect the appearance of original ideas and of knowledge than we can expect the propagation of the species from persons with completely stunted reproductive organs. On the other hand, a strong and beautifully developed build of the whole man, and especially of the brain, will certainly not in itself take the place of genius but it will at any rate supply the first and indispensable condition for higher knowledge."

Just as one ascribes to the human body the three forms of existence, mineral, plant and animal, so one must ascribe to it a fourth—the distinctively human form. Through his mineral existence man is related to everything visible; through his plantlike existence to all beings that grow and propagate their species; through his animal existence to all those that perceive their surroundings and by means of external impressions have inner experiences;

7

through his human form of existence he constitutes,
even in regard to his body alone, a kingdom by himself.

2. *The Soul Nature of Man*

Man's soul nature as his own inner world is different
from his bodily nature. When attention is turned to
even the simplest sensation, what is personally his own
comes at once to the fore. Thus no one can know whether
one person perceives even a simple sensation in exactly
the same way as another. It is known that there are people who are color-blind. They see things only in various
shades of grey. Others are only partially color-blind.
Because of this they are unable to distinguish between certain shades of color. The picture of the world that their
eyes gives them is different from that of so-called normal
persons. The same holds good more or less in regard to
the other senses. Thus it will be seen without further
elaboration that even simple sensations belong to the inner
world. I can perceive with my bodily senses the red table
that another person perceives but I cannot perceive his
sensation of red. We must, therefore, describe sensation
as belonging to the soul. If this single fact is grasped quite
clearly, we shall soon cease to regard inner experiences as
mere brain processes or something similar. Feeling must
link itself with sensation. One sensation causes us pleasure, another displeasure. These are stirrings of our inner
life, our soul life. In our feelings we create a second world

8

in addition to the one working on us from without. A third is added to this—the world of the will. Through the will we react on the outer world thereby stamping the impress of our inner being upon it. The soul of man, as it were, flows outwards in the activities of his will.

The actions of man differ from the occurrences of outer nature in that they bear the impress of his inner life. Thus the soul as man's own possession stands confronting the outer world. He receives from the outer world the incitements, but he creates in response to these incitements a world of his own. The body becomes the foundation of the soul being of man.

3. *The Spiritual Nature of Man*

The soul nature of man is not determined by the body alone. Man does not wander aimlessly and without purpose from one sensation to another, nor does he act under the influence of every casual incitement that plays upon him either from without or through the processes of his body. He thinks about his perceptions and his acts. By thinking about his perceptions he gains knowledge of things. By thinking about his acts he introduces a reasonable coherence into his life. He knows that he will worthily fulfill his duty as a man only when he lets himself be guided by correct thoughts in knowing as well as in acting. The soul of man, therefore, is confronted by a twofold necessity. By the laws of the body it is governed by natural necessity.

9

It allows itself also to be governed by the laws that guide it to exact thinking because it voluntarily acknowledges their necessity. Nature subjects man to the laws of changing matter, but he subjects himself to the laws of thought. By this means he makes himself a member of a higher order than the one to which he belongs through his body. This order is the spiritual. The spiritual is as different from the soul as the soul is from the body. As long as only the particles of carbon, hydrogen, nitrogen and oxygen that are in motion in the body are spoken of, we do not have the soul in view. Soul life begins only when within the motion of these particles the feeling arises, "I taste sweetness," or, "I feel pleasure." Likewise, we do not have the spirit in view as long as merely those soul experiences are considered that course through anyone who gives himself over entirely to the outer world and his bodily life. This soul life is rather the basis of the spiritual just as the body is the basis of the soul life. The biologist is concerned with the body, the investigator of the soul—the psychologist—with the soul, and the investigator of the spirit with the spirit. It is incumbent on those who would understand the nature of man by means of thinking, first to make clear to themselves through self-reflection the difference between body, soul and spirit.

4. Body, Soul and Spirit*

Man can only come to a true understanding of himself when he grasps clearly the significance of thinking within his being. The brain is the bodily instrument of thinking. A properly constructed eye serves us for seeing colors, and the suitably constructed brain serves us for thinking. The whole body of man is so formed that it receives its crown in the physical organ of the spirit, the brain. The construction of the human brain can only be understood by considering it in relation to its task—that of being the bodily basis for the thinking spirit. This is borne out by a comparative survey of the animal world. Among the amphibians the brain is small in comparison with the spinal cord; in mammals it is proportionately larger; in man it is largest in comparison with the rest of the body.

There are many prejudices prevalent regarding such statements about thinking as are presented here. Many people are inclined to under-value thinking and to place higher value on the warm life of feeling or emotion. Some even say it is not by sober thinking but by warmth of feeling and the immediate power of the emotions that we raise ourselves to higher knowledge. People who talk in this way are afraid they will blunt the feelings by clear thinking. This certainly does result from ordinary thinking that refers only to matters of utility. In the case of thoughts that lead to higher regions of existence, what happens is

---

* See *Addendum 3.*

11

just the opposite. There is no feeling and no enthusiasm to be compared with the sentiments of warmth, beauty and exaltation that are enkindled through the pure, crystal-clear thoughts that refer to the higher worlds. The highest feelings are, as a matter of fact, not those that come of themselves, but those that are achieved by energetic and persevering thinking.

The human body is so constructed that it is adapted to thinking. The same materials and forces that are present in the mineral kingdom are so combined in the human body that thought can manifest itself by means of this combination. This mineral structure built up in accordance with its function will be called in the following pages the *physical body* of man.

Organized with reference to the brain as its central point, this mineral structure comes into existence by propagation and reaches its fully developed form through growth. Man shares propagation and growth in common with plants and animals. Through propagation and growth what is living differentiates itself from the lifeless mineral. Life gives rise to life by means of the germ. Descendant follows forefather from one living generation to another. The forces through which a mineral originates are directed upon the substances of which it is composed. A quartz crystal is formed through the forces inherent in the silicon and oxygen that are combined in the crystal. The forces that shape an oak tree must be sought for indirectly in the germ-cells of the mother and father plants. The

12

form of the oak is preserved through propagation from forefather to descendant. Thus, there are inner determining conditions innate in living things, and it was a crude view of nature that held lower animals, even fishes, to have evolved out of mud. The form of the living passes itself on by means of heredity. How a living being develops depends on what father and mother it has sprung from—in other words, on the species to which it belongs. The materials it is composed of are continually changing but the species remains constant during life and is transmitted to the descendants. Therefore, it is the species that determines the combination of the materials. This force that determines species will here be called life-force. Mineral forces express themselves in crystals, and the formative life-force expresses itself in the species or forms of plant and animal life.

The mineral forces are perceived by man by means of his bodily senses, and he can only perceive things for which he has such senses. Without the eye there is no perception of light; without the ear no perception of sound. The lowest organisms have only one of the senses belonging to man—a kind of sense of touch.* These organisms have no awareness of the world perceptible to man with the exception of those mineral forces that they perceive by the sense of touch. In proportion to the development of the other senses in the higher animals does their surrounding world, which man also perceives,

---

* See *Addendum 2*.

13

become richer and more varied. It depends, therefore, on the organs of a being whether what exists in the outer world exists also for the being itself as something perceptible. What is present in the air as a certain motion becomes in man the sensation of hearing. Man, however, does not perceive the manifestations of the life-force through the ordinary senses. He sees the colors of the plants; he smells their perfume. The life-force, however, remains hidden from this form of observation. Even so, those with ordinary senses have just as little right to deny that there is a life-force as the man born blind has to deny that colors exist. Colors are there for the person born blind as soon as he has undergone an operation. In the same way, the various species of plants and animals created by the life-force—not merely the individual plants and animals—are present for man as objects of perception as soon as the necessary organ unfolds within him. An entirely new world opens out to him through the unfolding of this organ. He now perceives not merely the colors, the odors and other characteristics of living beings, but the life itself of these beings. In each plant and animal he perceives, besides the physical form, the life-filled spirit-form. In order to have a name for this spirit-form, let it be called the *ether body* or *life body*.*

----

* The author wishes to note that long after this book was written, he gave the name "formative-force body" to what is here called etheric or life body, (also cp. *Das Reich,* fourth book of the first year's issue, January, 1917). He felt himself moved to give it this name

14

To the investigator of spiritual life this ether body is for him not merely a product of the materials and forces of the physical body, but a real independent entity that first calls forth into life these physical materials and forces. We speak in accordance with spiritual science when we

---

because he believes that one cannot do enough to prevent the misunderstanding due to confusing what is here called etheric body with the "vital force" of older natural science. In what concerns the rejection of this older concept of a vital force in the sense of modern natural science, the author shares, in a certain sense, the standpoint of those who are opposed to assuming the existence of such a vital force. The purpose of assuming such a vital force was to explain how the inorganic forces work in a special way in the organism. But there is no difference between the activity of the inorganic in the organism and its activity outside in the inorganic world. The laws of inorganic nature are in the organism no different from what they are in the crystal. But in the organism there is present something that is not inorganic—the formative life. The etheric body, or formative force body, lies at the base of this formative life. By assuming its existence, the rightful task of natural science is not interfered with, namely, to observe the workings of forces in inorganic nature and to follow these workings into the organic world, and further, to refuse to think of these operations within the organism as being modified by a special vital force. To a true spiritual science this seems justified. The spiritual researcher speaks of the etheric body insofar as there manifests in the organism something different from what shows itself in the lifeless. In spite of all this, the author does not feel himself impelled to replace the term "etheric body" by the other "formative force body," since within the whole connected range of what is said here, any misunderstanding is excluded for anyone who really wants to comprehend. Such a misunderstanding can only arise when the term is used in a development that cannot exhibit this connection. (Compare this also with what is said under *Addendum 1*.)

15

say that a purely physical body derives its form—a crystal, for example—through the action of the physical formative forces innate in the lifeless. A living body does not receive its form through the action of these forces because in the moment life has departed from it and it is given over to the physical forces only, it falls to pieces. The ether body is an organism that preserves the physical body from dissolution every moment during life. In order to see this body, to perceive it in another being, the awakened *spiritual eye* is required. Without this ability its existence as a fact can still be accepted on logical grounds, but it can be seen with the spiritual eye just as color can be seen with the physical eye.

We should not take offense at the expression "ether body." "Ether" here designates something different from the hypothetical ether of the physicist. We should regard it simply as a name for what is described here. The structure of the physical body of the human being is a kind of reflection of its purpose, and this is also the case with the human etheric body. It can be understood only when it is considered in relation to the thinking spirit. The human etheric body differs from that of plants and animals through being organized to serve the purposes of the thinking spirit. Man belongs to the mineral world through his physical body, and he belongs through this etheric body to the life-world. After death the physical body dissolves into the mineral world, the ether body into the life-world. By the word "body" is meant whatever gives a being shape

16

or form. The term body must not be confused with a bodily form perceptible to the physical senses. Used in the sense implied in this book, the term body can also be applied to such forms as soul and spirit may assume.

The life-body is still something external to man. With the first stirrings of sensation the inner self responds to the stimuli of the outer world. You may search forever in what is called the outer world but you will be unable to find sensation in it. Rays of light stream into the eye, penetrating it until they reach the retina. There they cause chemical processes in the so-called visual-purple. The effect of these stimuli is passed on through the optic nerve to the brain. There further physical processes arise. Could these be observed, we would simply see more physical processes just as elsewhere in the physical world. If I am able also to observe the ether body, I shall see how the physical brain process is at the same time a life-process. The sensation of blue color that the recipient of the rays of light experiences, however, I can find nowhere in this manner. It arises only within the soul of the recipient. If, therefore, the being of this recipient consisted only of the physical and ether bodies, sensation could not exist. The activity by which sensation becomes a fact differs essentially from the operations of the formative life-force. By that activity an inner experience is called forth from these operations. Without this activity there would be a mere life-process such as we observe in plants. Imagine a man receiving impressions from all sides. Think of him

17

as the source of the activity mentioned above, flowing out in all directions from which he is receiving these impressions. In all directions sensations arise in response to the stimuli. This fountain of activity is to be called the *sentient soul*. This sentient soul is just as real as the physical body. If a man stands before me and I disregard his sentient soul by thinking of him as merely a physical body, it is exactly as if, instead of a painting, I were to call up in memory merely the canvas.

A statement similar to the one previously made in reference to the ether body must be made here about perceiving the sentient soul. The bodily organs are blind to it. The organ by which life can be perceived as life is also blind to it. The ether body is seen by means of this organ, and so through a still higher organ the inner world of sensation can become a special kind of supersensible perception. Then a man not only senses the impressions of the physical and life world, but he beholds the sensations themselves. The sensation world of another being is spread out before a man with such an organ like an external reality. One must distinguish between experiencing one's own sensation world, and looking at the sensation world of another person. Every man, of course, can see into his own sensation world. Only the seer with the opened spiritual eye can see the sensation world of another. Unless a man is a seer, he knows the world of sensation only as an inner one, only as the peculiar hidden experiences of his own soul. With the opened spiritual eye there shines out before the outward-turned spiritual gaze what otherwise lives only in the inner nature of another being.

*   *   *

In order to prevent misunderstanding, it may be expressly stated here that the seer does not experience in himself what the other being experiences as the content of his world of sensation. The other being experiences the sensations in question from the point of view of his own inner nature. The seer, however, becomes aware of a manifestation or expression of the sentient world.

The sentient soul's activity depends entirely on the ether body. The sentient soul draws from the ether body what it in turn causes to gleam forth as sensation. Since the ether body is the life within the physical body, the sentient soul is also directly dependent on the physical body. Only with correctly functioning and well-constructed eyes are correct color sensations possible. It is in this way that the nature of the body affects the sentient soul, and it is thus determined and limited in its activity by the body. It lives within the limitations fixed for it by the nature of the body. The body accordingly is built up of mineral substances, is vitalized by the ether body, and itself limits the sentient soul. A man, therefore, who has the organ mentioned above for seeing the sentient soul sees it limited by the body, but its limits do not coincide with those of the physical body. This soul extends some-what beyond the physical body and proves itself to be greater than the physical body. The force through which its limits are set, however, proceeds from the physical body. Thus, between the physical body and the ether body on the one hand, and the sentient soul on the other, another distinct member of the human constitution inserts itself. This is the *soul body* or sentient body. It may also be said that one part of the ether body is finer than the rest and this finer part forms a unity with the sentient soul, whereas the coarser part forms a kind of unity with the physical body. The sentient soul, nevertheless, extends, as has been said, beyond the soul body.

What is here called sensation is only a part of the soul nature. (The expression sentient soul is chosen for the sake of simplicity.) Connected with sensations are the feelings of desire and aversion, impulses, instincts, passions. All these bear the same character of individual life as do the sensations, and are, like them, dependent on the bodily nature.

*   *   *

The sentient soul enters into mutual action and reaction with the body, and also with thinking, with the spirit. In the first place, thinking serves the sentient soul. Man forms thoughts about his sensations and thus enlightens himself regarding the outside world. The child that has burnt itself thinks it over and reaches the thought, "Fire burns." Man does not follow his impulses, instincts and passions blindly but his reflection upon them brings about the opportunity for him to gratify them. What one calls material civilization is motivated entirely in this direction. It consists in the services that thinking renders to the sentient soul. Immeasurable quantities of thought-power are directed to this end. It is thought-power that has built ships, railways, telegraphs and telephones, and by far the greatest proportion of these conveniences serves only to satisfy the needs of sentient souls. Thought-force permeates the sentient soul similarly to the way the formative life-force permeates the physical body. The formative life-force connects the physical body with forefathers and descendants and thus brings it under a system of laws with which the purely mineral body is in no way concerned. In the same way thought-force brings the soul under a system of laws to which it does not belong as mere sentient soul. Through the sentient soul man is related to the animals. In animals also we observe the presence of sensations, impulses, instincts and passions. The animal, however, obeys these immediately and they do not become interwoven with independent thoughts thereby transcending the immediate experiences.* This is also the case to a certain extent with undeveloped human beings. The mere sentient soul, therefore, differs from the evolved higher member of the soul

---

* See *Addendum 4.*

that brings thinking into its service. This soul that is served by thought will be termed the *intellectual soul*. It could also be called the mind soul.

The intellectual soul permeates the sentient soul. The one who possesses the organ for seeing the soul sees the intellectual soul as a separate entity in contrast to the mere sentient soul.

*   *   *

By thinking, the human being is led above and beyond his own personal life. He acquires something that extends beyond his soul. He comes to take for granted his conviction that the laws of thought are in conformity with the laws of the universe, and he feels at home in the universe because this conformity exists. This conformity is one of the weighty facts through which he learns to know his own nature. He searches in his soul for truth, and through this truth it is not only the soul that speaks but also the things of the world. What is recognized as truth by means of thought has an independent significance that refers to the things of the world, and not merely to one's own soul. In my delight at the starry heavens I live in my own inner being. The thoughts I form for myself about the paths of heavenly bodies have the same significance for the thinking of every other person as they have for mine. It would be absurd to speak of my delight were I not in existence. It is not in the same way absurd, however, to speak of my thoughts, even without reference to myself, because the truth that I think today was true also yesterday and will be true tomorrow, although I concern myself with it only today. If a fragment of knowledge gives me joy, the joy has significance just as long as it lives in me, whereas the truth of the knowledge has its significance quite independently of this joy.

By grasping the truth, the soul connects itself with something that carries its value in itself. This value does not vanish with the feeling in the soul any more than it arose with it. What is really truth neither arises nor passes away. It has a significance that cannot be destroyed. This is not contradicted by the fact that certain human truths have a value that is transitory inasmuch as they are recognized after a certain period as partial or complete errors. Man must say to himself that truth after all exists in itself, although his conceptions are only transient forms of manifestation of the eternal truths. Even someone who says, like Lessing, that he contents himself with the eternal striving for truth because the full pure truth can only exist for a god, does not deny the eternity of truth but establishes it by such an utterance. Only what has an eternal significance in itself can call forth an eternal striving for it. Were truth not in itself independent, if it acquired its value and significance through the feelings of the human soul, it could not be the one unique goal for all mankind. By the very fact of our striving for truth, we concede its independent being.

As it is with the true, so is it with the truly good. Moral goodness is independent of inclinations and passions inasmuch as it does not allow itself to be commanded by them but commands them. Likes and dislikes, desire and loathing belong to the personal soul of a man. Duty stands higher than likes and dislikes. Duty may stand so high in the eyes of a man that he will sacrifice his life for its sake. A man stands the higher the more he has ennobled his inclinations, his likes and dislikes, so that without compulsion or subjection they themselves obey what is recognized as duty. The morally good has, like truth, its eternal value in itself and does not receive it from the sentient soul.

By causing the self-existent true and good to come to life in his inner being, man raises himself above the mere sentient soul. An imperishable light is kindled in it. In so far as the soul lives in this light, it is a participant in the eternal and unites its existence with it. What the soul carries within itself of the true and the good is immortal in it. Let us call what shines forth in the soul as eternal, the *consciousness soul*. We can speak of consciousness even in connection with the lower soul stirrings. The most ordinary everyday sensation is a matter of consciousness. To this extent animals also have consciousness. The kernel of human consciousness, that is, *the soul within the soul,* is what is here meant by consciousness soul. The consciousness soul is thus distinguished as a member of the soul distinct from the intellectual soul, which is still entangled in the sensations, impulses and passions. Everyone knows how a man at first counts as true what he prefers in his feelings and desires. Only that truth is permanent, however, that has freed itself from all flavor of such sympathy and antipathy of feeling. The truth is true even if all personal feelings revolt against it. That part of the soul in which this truth lives will be called consciousness soul.

Thus three members must be distinguished in the soul as in the body, namely, *sentient soul, intellectual soul* and *consciousness soul.* As the body works from below upwards with a limiting effect on the soul, so the spiritual works from above downwards into it, expanding it. The more the soul fills itself with the true and the good, the wider and the more comprehensive becomes the eternal in it. To him who is able to see the soul, the splendor radiating forth from a man in whom the eternal is expanding is just as much a reality as the light that streams out from a flame is real to the physical eye.

For the seer, the corporeal man counts as only part of the whole man. The physical body as the coarsest structure lies within others that mutually interpenetrate it and each other. The ether body fills the physical body as a life-form. The soul body (astral shape) can be perceived extending beyond this on all sides. Beyond this, again, extends the sentient soul, and then the intellectual soul, which grows the larger the more of the true and the good it receives into tself. This true and good causes the

25

expansion of the intellectual soul. On the other hand, a man living only and entirely according to his inclinations, likes and dislikes, would have an intellectual soul whose limits coincide with those of his sentient soul. These organizations, in the midst of which the physical body appears as if in a cloud, may be called the *human aura*. The perception of this aura, when seen as this book endeavors to present it, indicates an enrichment of man's soul nature.

* * *

In the course of his development as a child, there comes the moment in the life of a man when for the first time he feels himself to be an independent being distinct from all the rest of the world. For sensitive natures, it is a significant experience. The poet, Jean Paul, says in his autobiography, "I shall never forget the event that took place within me, hitherto narrated to no one and of which I can give place and time, when I stood present at the birth of my self-consciousness. As a small child I stood one morning at the door of the house looking towards the wood-pile on my left, when suddenly the inner vision, I am an I, came upon me like a flash of lightning from heaven and has remained shining ever since. In that moment my ego had seen itself for the first time and forever. Any deception of memory is hardly to be conceived as possible here, for no narrations by outsiders could have

26

introduced additions to an occurrence that took place in the holy of holies of a human being, and of which the novelty alone gave permanence to such everyday surroundings." It is known that little children say of themselves, "Charles is good," "Mary wants to have this." One feels it to be right that they speak of themselves as if of others because they have not yet become conscious of their independent existence, and the consciousness of the self is not yet born in them.*

Through self-consciousness man describes himself as an independent being separate from all others, as "I." In his "I" he brings together all that he experiences as a being with body and soul. Body and soul are the carriers of the ego or "I," and in them it acts. Just as the physical body has its center in the brain, so has the soul its center in the ego. Man is aroused to sensations by impacts from without; feelings manifest themselves as effects of the outer world; the will relates itself to the outside world, realizing itself in external actions. The "I" as the particular and essential being of man remains quite invisible. With excellent judgment, therefore, does Jean Paul call a man's recognition of his ego an "occurrence taking place only in the veiled holy of holies of a human being," for with his "I" man is quite alone. This "I" is the very man himself. That justifies him in regarding his ego as his true being. He may, therefore, describe his body and his soul as the sheaths or veils within

* See *Addendum 5.*

which he lives, and he may describe them as bodily conditions through which he acts. In the course of his evolution he learns to regard these tools ever more as instruments of service to his ego. The little word "I" is a name which differs from all others. Anyone who reflects in an appropriate manner on the nature of this name will find that in so doing an avenue opens itself to the understanding of the human being in the deeper sense. Any other name can be applied to its corresponding object by all men in the same way. Anybody can call a table, table, or a chair, chair. This is not so with the name "I." No one can use it in referring to another person. Each one can call only himself "I." Never can the name "I" reach my ears from outside when it refers to me. Only from within, only through itself, can the soul refer to itself as "I." When man therefore says "I" to himself, something begins to speak in him that has to do with none of the worlds from which the sheaths so far mentioned are taken. The "I" becomes increasingly the ruler of body and soul.

This also expresses itself in the aura. The more the "I" is lord over body and soul, the more definitely organized, the more varied and the more richly colored is the aura. The effect of the "I" on the aura can be seen by the seer. The "I" itself is invisible even to him. This remains truly within the "veiled holy of holies of a human being." The "I" absorbs into itself the rays of the light that flame forth in him as eternal light. As he gathers together the experiences of body and soul in the "I," so too he causes the thoughts of truth and goodness to stream into the "I." The phenomena of the senses reveal themselves to the "I" from the one side, the spirit reveals itself from the other. Body and soul yield themselves up to the "I" in order to serve it, but the "I" yields itself up to the spirit in order that the spirit may fill it to overflowing. The "I" lives in body and soul, but the spirit lives in the "I." What there is of spirit in it is eternal, for the "I" receives its nature and significance from that with which it is bound up. In so far as it lives in the physical body, it is subject to the laws of the mineral world; through its ether body to the laws of propagation and growth; by virtue of the sentient and intellectual souls, to the laws of the soul world; in so far as it receives the spiritual into itself it is subject to the laws of the spirit. What the laws of mineral and of life construct, comes into being and vanishes. The spirit has nothing to do with becoming and perishing.

*　　*　　*

The "I" lives in the soul. Although the highest manifestation of the "I" belongs to the consciousness soul, one must, nevertheless, say that this "I" raying out from it fills the whole of the soul, and through it exerts its action upon the body. In the "I" the spirit is alive. The spirit sends its rays into the "I" and lives in it as in a sheath or veil, just as the "I" lives in its sheaths, the body and soul. The spirit develops the "I" from within, outwards; the mineral world develops it from without, inwards. The spirit forming and living as "I" will be called *spirit self* because it manifests as the "I," or ego, or self of man. The difference between the spirit self and the consciousness soul can be made clear in the following way. The consciousness soul is in touch with the self-existent truth that is independent of all antipathy and sympathy. The spirit self bears within it the same truth, but taken up into and enclosed by the "I," individualized by it, and absorbed into the independent being of the individual. It is through the eternal truth becoming thus individualized and bound up into one being with the "I" that the "I" itself attains to the eternal.

The spirit self is a revelation of the spiritual world within the "I," just as from the other side sensations are a revelation of the physical world within the "I." In what is red, green, light, dark, hard, soft, warm, cold one recognizes the revelations of the corporeal world. In what is true and good are to be found the revelations of the spiritual world. In the same sense in which the revelation of the corporeal world is called sensation, let the revelation of the spiritual be called intuition.* Even the most simple thought contains intuition because one cannot touch thought with the hands or see it with the eyes. Its revela-

* See *Addendum 6*.

30

tion must be received from the spirit through the "I." If an undeveloped and a developed man look at a plant, there lives in the ego of the one something quite different from what exists in the ego of the other. Yet the sensation of both are called forth by the same object. The difference lies in this, that the one can form far more perfect thoughts about the object than the other. If objects revealed themselves through sensation only, there could be no progress in spiritual development. Even the savage is affected by nature, but the laws of nature reveal themselves only to the thoughts fructified by intuition of the more highly developed man. The stimuli from the outer world are felt also by the child as incentives to the will, but the commandments of the morally good disclose themselves to him in the course of his development in proportion as he learns to live in the spirit and understand its revelations.

There could be no color sensations without physical eyes, and there could be no intuitions without the higher thinking of the spirit self. As little as sensation creates the plant in which color appears does intuition create the spiritual realities about which it is merely giving knowledge.

The ego of a man that comes to life in the soul draws into itself messages from above, from the spirit world, through intuitions, and through sensations it draws in messages from the physical world. In so doing it makes the spirit world into the individualized life of its own soul, even as it does the physical world by means of the senses. The soul, or rather the "I" flaming forth in it, opens its portals on two sides—towards the corporeal and towards the spiritual.

Now the physical world can only give information about itself to the ego by building out of physical materials and forces a body in which the conscious soul can live and possess within it organs for perceiving the corporeal world outside itself. The spiritual world, on the other hand, with its spiritual substances and spiritual forces, builds a spirit body in which the "I" can live and, through intuitions, perceive the spiritual. (It is evident that the expressions spirit substance, spirit body, contain contradictions according to the literal meaning of the words. They are only used to direct attention to what, in the spiritual region, corresponds to the physical substance, the physical body of a man.)

Within the physical world each human body is built up as a separate being, and within the spirit world the spirit body is also built up separately. For man there is an inner and an outer in the spirit world just as in the physical world there is an inner and an outer. Man takes in the materials of the physical world around him and assimilates them in his physical body, and he also takes up the spiritual from the spiritual environment and makes it into his own. The spiritual is the eternal nourishment of man. Man is born of the physical world, and he is

32

also born of the spirit through the eternal laws of the true and the good. He is separated as an independent being from the spirit world outside him, and he is separated in the same manner from the whole physical world. This independent spiritual being will be called the *spirit man.*

If we investigate the human physical body, it is found to contain the same materials and forces as are to be found outside in the rest of the physical world. It is the same with the spirit man. In it pulsate the elements of the external spirit world. In it the forces of the rest of the spirit world are active. Within the physical skin a being is enclosed and limited that is alive and feels. It is the same in the spirit world. The spiritual skin that separates the spirit man from the unitary spirit world makes him an independent being within it, living a life within himself and perceiving intuitively the spiritual content of the world. Let us call this "spiritual skin" (auric sheath) the *spirit sheath.* Only it must be kept clearly in mind that the spiritual skin expands continually with advancing human evolution so that the spiritual individuality of man (his auric sheath) is capable of enlargement to an unlimited extent.

The spirit man lives within this spirit sheath. It is built up by the spiritual life force in the same way as the physical body is by the physical life force. In a similar way to that in which one speaks of an ether body, one must speak of an ether spirit in reference to the spirit

33

man. Let this ether spirit be called *life spirit*. The spiritual nature of man is thus composed of three parts, *spirit man, life spirit* and *spirit self*.

For one who is a seer in the spiritual regions, this spiritual nature of man is, as the higher, truly spiritual part of the aura, a perceptible reality. He sees the spirit man as life spirit within the spirit sheath, and he sees how this life spirit grows continually larger by taking in spiritual nourishment from the spiritual external world. Further, he sees how the spirit sheath continually increases, widens out through what is brought into it, and how the spirit man becomes ever larger and larger. In so far as this becoming larger is seen spatially, it is of course only a picture of the reality. This fact notwithstanding, the human soul is directed towards the corresponding spiritual reality in conceiving this picture because the difference between the spiritual and the physical nature of man is that the physical nature has a limited size while the spiritual nature can grow to an unlimited extent.

Whatever of spiritual nourishment is absorbed has an eternal value. The human aura is accordingly composed of two interpenetrating parts. Color and form are given to the one by the physical existence of a man, and to the other by his spiritual existence. The ego marks the separation between them in such wise that the physical element after its own manner surrenders itself and builds up a body that allows a soul to live within it. The "I" surrenders itself and allows the spirit to develop in it, which now for its part permeates the soul and gives the soul its goal in the spirit world. Through the body the soul is enclosed in the physical. Through the spirit man there grow wings for movement in the spiritual world.

*   *   *

In order to comprehend the whole man one must think of him as put together out of the components mentioned above. The body builds itself up out of the world of physical matter in such a way that this structure is adapted to the requirements of the thinking ego. It is permeated with life force and becomes thereby the etheric or life body. As such it opens itself through the sense organs towards the outer world and becomes the soul body. The sentient soul permeates this and becomes a unity with it. The sentient soul does not merely receive the impacts of the outer world as sensations. It has its own inner life, fertilized through thinking on the one hand and through sensations on the other. The sentient soul thus becomes the intellectual soul. It is able to do this by opening itself to the intuitions from above as it does to sensations from below. Thus it becomes the consciousness soul. This is possible because the spirit world builds into it the organ of intuition, just as the physical body builds for it the sense organs. The senses transmit sensations by means of the soul body, and the spirit transmits to it intuitions through the organ of intuition. The spiritual human being is thereby linked into a unity with the consciousness soul, just as the physical body is linked with the sentient soul in the soul body. Consciousness soul and spirit self form a unity. In this unity the spirit man lives as life spirit in the same way that the ether body forms the bodily life basis for the soul body. Thus, as the physical body is enclosed in the physical skin, so is the spirit man in the spirit sheath. The members of the whole man are therefore as follows:

A. Physical body.
B. Ether or life body.
C. Soul body.
D. Sentient soul.
E. Intellectual soul.
F. Consciousness soul.
G. Spirit self.
H. Life spirit.
I. Spirit man.

Soul body (C) and sentient soul (D) are a unity in the earthly human being. In the same way consciousness soul (F) and spirit self (G) are a unity. Thus there come to be seven members in earthly man.

1. Physical body.
2. Etheric or life body.
3. Sentient soul body.

36

4. Intellectual soul.
5. Spirit-filled consciousness soul.
6. Life spirit.
7. Spirit man.

In the soul the "I" flashes forth, receives the impulse from the spirit, and thereby becomes the bearer of the spiritual human being. Thus man participates in the three worlds, the physical, the soul and the spiritual. He is rooted in the physical world through his physical body, ether body and soul body, and through the spirit self, life spirit and spirit man he comes to flower in the spiritual world. The stalk, however, that takes root in the one and flowers in the other is the soul itself.

This arrangement of the members of man can be expressed in a simplified way, but one entirely consistent with the above. Although the human "I" flashes forth in the consciousness soul, it nevertheless penetrates the whole soul being. The parts of this soul being are not at all as distinctly separate as are the members of the bodily nature. They interpenetrate each other in a higher sense. If then one regards the intellectual soul and the consciousness soul as the two sheaths of the "I" that belong together, with the "I" itself as their kernel, then one can divide man into physical body, life body, astral body and "I." The expression astral body designates what is formed by considering the soul body and sentient soul as a unity. This expression is found in the older literature, and may be applied here in a somewhat broad sense to what lies beyond the sensibly perceptible in the constitution of man. Although the sentient soul is in certain respects energized by the "I," it is still so intimately connected with the soul body that a single expression is justified when united. When now the "I" saturates itself with the spirit self, this spirit self makes its appearance in such a way that the astral body is transmuted from within the soul. In the astral body the impulses, desires and passions of man are primarily active in so far as they are felt by him. Sense perceptions also are active therein. Sense perceptions arise through the soul body as a member in man that comes to him from the external world. Impulses, desires and passions arise in the sentient soul in so far as it is energized from within, before this inner part has yielded itself to the spirit self. If the "I" saturates itself with the spirit self, then the soul energizes the astral body with this spirit self. This expresses itself in the illumination of the impulses, desires and passions by what the "I" has received from the spirit. The "I" has then, through its participation in the spiritual world, become ruler in the world of impulses and desires. To the extent to which it has become this, the spirit self manifests in the astral body, and the astral body is transmuted thereby. The astral body itself then appears as a two-fold body—partly untransmuted and partly transmuted. We can, therefore, designate the spirit self manifesting itself in man as the transmuted astral body.

38

A similar process takes place in the human individual when he receives the life spirit into his "I." The life body then becomes transmuted, penetrated with the life spirit. The life spirit manifests itself in such a way that the life body becomes quite different from what it was. For this reason it can also be said that the life spirit is the transmuted life body. If the "I" receives the spirit man, it thereby receives the necessary force to penetrate the physical body. Naturally, that part of the physical body thus transmuted is not perceptible to the physical senses, because it is just this spiritualized part of the physical body that has become the spirit man. It is then present to the physical senses as physical, and insofar as this physical is spiritualized, it has to be beheld by spiritual perceptive faculties, because to the external senses the physical, even when penetrated by the spiritual, appears to be merely sensible.

Taking all this as basis, the following arrangement may also be given of the members of man:

1. Physical body.
2. Life body.
3. Astral body.
4. I, as soul kernel.
5. Spirit self as transmuted astral body.
6. Life spirit as transmuted life body.
7. Spirit man as transmuted physical body.

Chapter II

RE-EMBODIMENT OF THE SPIRIT AND DESTINY *

THE soul lives between body and spirit. The impressions coming to it through the body are transitory, enduring only as long as the body opens its organs to the things of the outer world. Only while the rose is in my line of vision can my open eye perceive its color. The presence of the things of the outer world as well as of the bodily organs is necessary in order that an impression, a sensation or a perception can occur. But what I have recognized in my mind as truth concerning the rose does not pass with the present moment, and as regards its truth, it is not in the least dependent on me. It would be true even though I had never stood before the rose. What I know through the spirit is rooted in an element of the soul life through which the soul is linked with a world-content that manifests itself in the soul independent of its bodily basis. The point here is not whether what manifests itself is essentially imperishable, but whether the

* See *Addendum 7*.

manifestation occurs for the soul in such a way that its perishable bodily basis plays no part, and only that plays a part in it that is independent of this perishable body. The enduring element in the soul comes under observation at the moment we become aware that the soul has experiences not limited by its perishable factor. Again the important point is not whether these experiences come to consciousness primarily through perishable processes of the bodily organization, but the fact that they contain something that does indeed live in the soul, yet is independent of the transient process of perception. The soul is placed between the present and duration in that it holds the middle place between body and spirit. It also mediates between the present and duration. It preserves the present for remembrance, thus rescuing it from impermanence by taking it up into the duration of its own spiritual being. It also stamps what endures upon the temporal and impermanent by not merely yielding itself up in its own life to the transitory incitements, but by determining things out of its own initiative and embodying its own nature in them in the shape of the actions it performs. By remembrance the soul preserves the yesterday; by action it prepares the tomorrow.

If my soul could not retain the red of the rose through remembrance, it would always have to perceive it anew to be conscious of it. What can be retained by the soul after an external impression can become a mental image, independent of the external impression. Through this power of forming visualizations the soul makes the outer world so much its own inner world that it can then retain the latter in memory for remembrance and, independent of the impressions acquired, lead a life of its own with it. The soul life thus becomes the enduring effect of the transitory impressions of the external world.

Action also receives permanence when once it is stamped on the outer world. If I cut a twig from a tree, something has taken place through my soul that completely changes the course of events in the outer world. Something quite different would have happened to the branch of the tree had I not interfered by my action. I have called into life a series of effects that, without my existence, would not have been present. What I have done today endures for tomorrow. Through the deed it acquires permanence just as my impressions of yesterday have become permanent for my soul through memory.

For this fact of creating permanence through action we do not, in our ordinary consciousness, form a definite visualization such as we have for memory, or as the result of a perception of an experience made permanent. Is not the ego of a man, however, linked just as much to the alteration in the world resulting from the deed as it is to a memory resulting from an impression? The ego judges new impressions differently depending upon whether or not it has one or another recollection. It has also as an "I" entered into a different relation to the world according to whether or not it has performed one deed or another.

42

Whether, in the relation between the world and my "I," a certain new quality is present or not depends upon whether or not I have made an impression on another person through my action. I am quite a different person in my relationship to the world after having made an impression on my surroundings.

The fact that what is meant here is not so generally noticed as is the change taking place in the ego through its having acquired a recollection, is solely due to the circumstances that the moment a recollection is formed it unites itself with the soul life that man has always felt to be his own. The external effects of the deed, detached from this soul life, produce consequences that are again something quite different from what the memory retains of this deed. Apart from this, it must be admitted that after a deed has been accomplished, there is something in the world upon which the ego has stamped its character. If we really think out what is here being considered, the question must arise as to whether the results of a deed, on which the "I" has stamped its own nature, retain a tendency to return to the "I" just as an impression preserved in the memory is revived in response to some external inducement. What is preserved in the memory waits for such an inducement. Is it not possible that what has retained the imprint of the ego in the external world waits also to approach the human soul from without, just as memory, in response to a given inducement, approaches it from within? This matter is only put forward here as a

43

question because it certainly might happen that the occasion would never arise on which the consequences of a deed, bearing the impress of the ego, could take effect in the human soul. That these consequences are present as such, and that through their presence they determine the relation of the world to the "I," is seen at once to be a possibility when we really follow out in thought the matter before us. In the following considerations we shall inquire whether there is anything in human life that, starting from this possibility, points to a reality.

*   *   *

Let us first consider memory. How does it originate? Evidently in quite a different way from sensation or perception. Without the eye I cannot have the sensation blue, but by means of the eye alone I do not have the remembrance of blue. If the eye is to give me this sensation now, a blue object must stand before it. The body would allow all impressions to sink back again into oblivion were it not for the fact that while the present image is being formed through the act of perception, something is also taking place in the relationship between the outer world and the soul. This activity brings about certain results within man enabling him through processes within himself to form a new image of what, in the first place, was brought about by an image from outside. Anyone who has acquired practice in observing the life of the soul will

44

see the opinion to be quite erroneous that holds that the perception a man has today is the same he recalls tomorrow through memory, it having meanwhile remained somewhere or other within him. No, the perception I now have is a phenomenon that passes away with the "now." When recollection occurs, a process takes place in me that is the result of something that happened in the relation between the external world and me quite apart from the arousing of the present visualization. The mental image called forth through remembrance is not an old preserved visualization, but a new one. Recollection consists in the fact, not that a visualization can be revived, but that we can present to ourselves again and again what has been perceived. What reappears is something different from the original visualization. This remark is made here because in the domain of spiritual science it is necessary that more accurate conceptions should be formed than is the case in ordinary life, and indeed also in ordinary science.

I remember; that is, I experience something that is itself no longer present. I unite a past experience with my present life. This is the case with every remembrance. Let us say, for instance, that I meet a man and, because I met him yesterday, recognize him. He would be a complete stranger to me if I were unable to unite the picture that I made yesterday through my perception with my impression of him today. Today's image of him is given me through my perception, that is to say, through my sense organs. Who, then, conjures up yesterday's picture

45

in my soul? It is conjured up by the same being in me that was present during my experience yesterday, and that is also present today. In the previous explanations this being has been called soul. Were it not for this faithful preserver of the past, each external impression would always be new to us. It is certain that the soul imprints upon the body, as though by means of a sign, the process through which something becomes a recollection. Yet it is the soul itself that must make this impression and then perceive what it has made, just as it perceives something external. Thus the soul is the preserver of memory.

As preserver of the past, the soul continually gathers treasures for the spirit. That I can distinguish between what is correct or incorrect depends on the fact that I, as a man, am a thinking being able to grasp the truth in my spirit. Truth is eternal, and it could always reveal itself to me again in things even if I were to lose sight of the past and each impression were to be a new one to me. The spirit within me, however, is not restricted to the impressions of the present alone. The soul extends the spirit's horizon over the past, and the more the soul is able to bring to the spirit out of the past, the more does it enrich the spirit. The soul thus hands on to the spirit what it has received from the body. The spirit of man, therefore, carries at each moment of its life a twofold possession within itself. Firstly, the eternal laws of the good and the true, and secondly, the remembrance of the experiences of the past. What the human spirit does is accomplished under the influence of these two factors. If we want to understand a human spirit we must, therefore, know two different things about it. Firstly, how much of the eternal has been revealed to it, and secondly, how much treasure from the past lies stored up within it.

These treasures by no means remain in the spirit in an unchanged shape. The impressions that man acquires from his experiences fade gradually from memory. Not so, however, their fruits. We do not remember all the experiences lived through during childhood while acquiring the arts of reading and writing. Yet we could not read or write had we not had such experiences, and had not their fruits been preserved in the form of abilities. Such is the transmutation that the spirit effects in the treasures of memory. The spirit consigns to its fate whatever can lead to pictures of the separate experiences, and extracts therefrom only the force necessary for enhancing its abilities. Thus not a single experience passes by unutilized. The soul preserves each one as memory, and from each the spirit draws forth all that can enrich its abilities and the whole content of its life. The human spirit grows through assimilated experiences, and although one cannot find past experiences in the spirit as if in a storeroom, one nevertheless finds their effects in the abilities that man has acquired.

*   *   *

Thus far spirit and soul have been considered only within the period lying between birth and death. We cannot stop there. Anyone wishing to do so would be like the man who would observe the human body only within these same limits. Much can certainly be discovered within these limits, but the human form can never be explained by what lies between birth and death. It cannot build itself up directly out of mere physical substances and forces. It can only descend from a form like its own that arises as the result of what has handed itself on by heredity. The physical materials and forces build up the body during life. The forces of propagation enable another body, a body with a like form, to proceed from it— that is to say, one able to be the bearer of the same life body. Each life body is a repetition of its forebear. Only because it is such does it appear, not in any chance form, but in that passed on to it by heredity. The forces that make possible my human form lay in my forefathers.

The spirit of a man also appears in a definite form, and these forms of spiritual man are the most varied imaginable. In saying this, the word form is naturally used in a spiritual sense. No two human beings have the same spiritual form. Observations should be made in this region in a manner just as quietly and matter-of-factly as they would be made in the physical world. It cannot be said that the differences in man in spiritual respects arise only from the differences in their environment and their upbringing. No, this is by no means the case because two people under similar influences of environment and upbringing develop in quite different ways. We are, there-

48

fore, forced to admit that they have entered on their paths of life with quite different dispositions. Here we are brought face to face with an important fact that sheds light on the nature of man when its full bearing is recognized.

Anyone who is set upon directing his outlook exclusively towards the side of material happenings could, indeed, assert that the individual differences of human personalities arise from differences in the constitution of the material germs. In view of the laws of heredity discovered by Gregor Mendel and developed further by others, such a claim can offer much that gives it the appearance of justification even in scientific judgments. Such judgment only shows, however, that these people have no insight into the real relation of man to his experiences. Careful observation shows that external circumstances affect different people in different ways because of something that by no means enters immediately into mutual relations with material development. To the really accurate researcher in this domain it becomes apparent that what proceeds from the material basis can be distinguished from what arises through the mutual interaction between a man and his experiences, although these experiences can only take shape and form through the participation of the soul itself in this mutual interaction. The soul stands there clearly in relation to something within the external world that, by virtue of its very nature, cannot be connected with the material germinal basis.

Men differ from their animal fellow-creatures on earth

49

through their physical form, but regarding this form they are, within certain limits, like one another. There is only one human species. However great may be the differences between races, people, tribes and personalities, as regards the physical body, the resemblance between man and man is greater than between man and any animal species. All that finds expression in the human species is conditioned by the inheritance of descendants from forebears, and the human form is bound to this heredity. As the lion can inherit its physical bodily form from lion forebears only, so can man inherit his physical bodily form only from human forebears.

The physical similarity of men is apparent to our physical eyes, and the differences of their spiritual forms lie revealed to our unbiased spiritual gaze. There is one fact that shows this clearly—the existence of a man's biography. Were a man merely a member of a species, no biography could exist. A lion or a dove are interesting insofar as they belong to the lion or the dove species. The separate being in all its essentials has been understood when the species has been described. It matters little whether one has to do with father, son or grandson. What they have of interest in them, father, son and grandson have in common. What a man signifies, however, is found only in his individuality, not in his being merely a member of a species. I have not in the least understood the nature of Mr. Smith of Hoboken if I have described his son or his father. I must know his own biography. Anyone who reflects on the nature of biography realizes that regarding the spiritual each man is himself a species.

To be sure, those people who regard a biography merely as a collection of external incidents in the life of an individual may claim they can write the biography of a dog in the same way they can that of a man. But anyone who depicts in a biography the real individuality of a man grasps the fact that he has in the biography of a single man something that corresponds to the description of a whole species in the animal kingdom. The point is obviously not that we can say something in the nature of a biography about an animal—especially clever ones. The point is that the human biography does not correspond to a biography of an animal, but to the description of the animal species. Of course, there will always be people who will seek to refute this by urging that owners of menageries, for instance, know how single animals of the same species differ individually from one another. The man who judges in this way, however, shows only that he is unable to distinguish individual difference from difference that is acquired only through individuality.

Now if genus or species in the physical sense becomes intelligible only when we understand it as conditioned by heredity, so, too, the spiritual being can be understood only through a similar spiritual heredity. I have received my physical human form because of my descent from human forebears, but whence have I received what finds expression in my biography? As physical man, I repeat

51

the shape of my forebears. What do I repeat as spiritual man? Anyone who claims that what comprises my biography needs no further explanation but must be accepted just as it stands, is also forced to maintain that he has seen an earth-mound somewhere on which lumps of matter have integrated themselves quite unaided into a living man.

As physical man I spring from other physical men because I have the same shape as the whole human species. The qualities of the species, accordingly, could thus be acquired only within the species. As spiritual man I have my own shape just as I have my own biography. I can have obtained this shape, therefore, from no one but myself. I did not enter the world with undefined, but with defined soul-predispositions, and since the course of my life as it comes to expression in my biography is determined by these predispositions, my work upon myself cannot have begun with my birth. That is to say, I must have existed as spiritual man before my birth. I certainly did not exist in my forebears because as spiritual human beings, they differ from me. My biography is not explainable through theirs. On the contrary, as a spiritual being I must be the repetition of someone through whose biography mine can be explained. The only conceivable alternative at the moment would be that I owe the character of the content of my biography to a spiritual life in which I existed prior to birth or, more correctly, to conception. We should, however, only be allowed to hold

52

this opinion if we are willing to assume that what acts upon the human soul from its physical surroundings is of the same nature as that which affects the soul from a purely spiritual world. Such an assumption contradicts really accurate observation because the effect of its physical environment on the human soul is like the impression made by a new experience on a similar past experience in the same life.

In order to observe these relations correctly, one must acquire a perception of the impressions operating in human life, whose influence upon the predispositions of the soul is like that of standing before a deed that has to be done, and that is related to what has already been experienced in physical life. But the soul does not bring faculties gained in this immediate life to meet these impressions, but predispositions, which receive the impressions in the same way as do the faculties acquired through practice. He who has insight into these matters arrives at the conception of earth-lives that must have preceded this present one. In his thinking he cannot stop at purely spiritual experiences that preceded this present earth-life. The physical form that Schiller bore was inherited from his forebears. In the same way that it was impossible for Schiller's physical form to have grown out of the earth, it was also impossible for his spiritual being to have originated from it. He must have been the repetition of another spiritual being through whose biography his own becomes explicable as his physical human form is

53

explicable through human propagation. In the same way, therefore, that the physical human form is again and again a repetition, a reincarnation of a being of the human species, so too the spiritual man must be a reincarnation of the same spiritual man, since, as spiritual man, each individual is, in fact, his own species.

The objection might be made that what has been stated here is a mere spinning of thoughts, and external proofs might be demanded as are customary in ordinary natural science. The reply to this is that the re-embodiment of the spiritual man is, naturally, a process that does not belong to the domain of external physical facts, but is one that takes place entirely in the spiritual region. No other of our ordinary powers of intelligence has entrance to this region save that of thinking. A person who will not trust the power of thinking cannot in fact enlighten himself regarding higher spiritual facts. For the one whose spiritual eye is opened, the above trains of thought act with exactly the same force as does an event that takes place before his physical eyes. The individual who ascribes to a so-called "proof," constructed according to the methods of natural science, greater power to convince than the above observations concerning the significance of biography, may be in the ordinary sense of the word a great scientist, but he is far from the paths of true spiritual research.

One of the most dangerous assumptions at present consists in trying to explain the spiritual qualities of a man by hereditary transmission from father, mother or other ancestors. Anyone who holds the opinion, for example, that Goethe inherited what constitutes his essential being from his father or mother will at first be hardly accessible to argument because there lies within such a one a deep antipathy to unprejudiced observation. A materialistic spell prevents him from seeing the mutual connections of phenomena in their true light.

In such observations as the above, the presuppositions are supplied for following man beyond birth and death. Within the boundaries formed by birth and death, man belongs to the worlds of physical body, of soul, and of spirit. The soul forms the intermediate link between body and spirit, inasmuch as it endows the third member of the body, the soul body, with the capacity for sensation, and inasmuch as it permeates the first member of the spirit, the spirit self, as consciousness soul. Thus it takes part and lot during life with the body as well as with the spirit. This comes to expression in its whole existence. How the sentient soul can unfold its capabilities will depend on the organization of the soul body. On the other hand, the extent to which the spirit self can develop itself within the consciousness soul will depend on the life of that soul. The more highly organized the soul body, the more complete the intercourse that the sentient soul can develop with the outer world. The spirit self will become that much richer and more powerful the more the consciousness soul brings nourishment to it. It has been shown that during life this nourishment is supplied to the spirit self through assimilated experiences and the fruits of these experiences. The interaction of the soul and spirit described above can, of course, only take place where soul and spirit are within each other, interpenetrating each other, that is, within the union of spirit self with consciousness soul.

Let us consider first the interaction of the soul body and the sentient soul. It is evident that the soul body is the most finely elaborated part of the body. Nevertheless, the soul body belongs to it and is dependent upon it. In a certain sense, physical body, ether body and soul body compose a single whole. Hence the soul body is also drawn within the laws of physical heredity that give the body its shape. Since it is the most mobile and volatile form of body, it must also exhibit the most mobile and volatile manifestations of heredity. Therefore, while the difference in the physical body corresponding to races, peoples and tribes is the smallest, and while in general the ether body presents a preponderating likeness and in single individuals a greater divergence, in the soul body the difference is already a considerable one. In it is expressed what is felt to be the external, personal uniqueness of an individual. Thus, it is also the bearer of that part of this personal uniqueness that is passed on from parents, grandparents, and so forth, to their descendants. As has been explained, it is true that the soul as such leads a completely self-contained life of its own in shutting itself up with its inclinations and disinclinations, its feelings and passions. It is nevertheless active as a whole and this whole comes to expression also in the sentient soul. Because the sentient soul interpenetrates and fills up the soul body, the latter forms itself according to the nature of the soul and can in this way, as the bearer of heredity, pass on tendencies, passions and other qualities from forefathers to children.

On this fact rests the statement of Goethe, "From my father I have stature and the serious manner of life; from my mother, a joyous disposition and the love of romance." Genius, of course, he did not receive from either. In this way we are shown what part of a man's soul qualities he hands over, as it were, to the line of physical heredity. The substances and forces of the physical body are in like manner present in the whole sphere of external physical nature. They are continually being taken up from it and given back to it. In the space of a few years the matter that composes our physical body is entirely renewed. That this matter takes the form of the human body, and that it always renews itself again within this body, depends upon the fact that it is held together by the ether body. The form of the ether body is not determined by events between birth or conception, and death alone, but is dependent on the laws of heredity that extend beyond birth and death. That soul qualities also can be transmitted by heredity—that the process of physical heredity receives an infusion from the soul—is due to the fact that the soul body can be influenced by the sentient soul.

57

Now, how does the interaction between soul and spirit proceed? During life, the spirit is bound up with the soul in the way shown above. The soul receives from the spirit the gift of living within the good and the true, and thereby of bringing the spirit itself to expression within its own life, within its tendencies, impulses and passions. From the world of the spirit, the spirit self brings to the "I" the eternal laws of the true and the good. These link themselves through the consciousness soul with the experiences of the soul's own life. These experiences themselves pass away, but their fruits remain. The spirit self receives an abiding impression by having been linked with them. When the human spirit encounters an experience similar to one to which it has already been linked, it sees therein something familiar, and is able to take up an attitude towards it quite different from what would be the case were the spirit facing it for the first time. This is the basis of all learning. The fruits of learning are acquired capacities. The fruits of the transitory life are in this way graven on the eternal spirit. Do we not see these fruits? Whence spring the innate predispositions and talents described above as characteristic of the spiritual man? Surely only from capacities of one kind or another that a man brings with him when he begins his earthly life. In certain respects, these capacities resemble exactly those that we can also acquire for ourselves during life.

Take the case of a genius. It is known that the boy Mozart could write out from memory a long musical work

58

after only one hearing. He was able to do this because he could survey the whole at once. Within certain limits a man is also able during life to increase his capacity of rapid survey, of grasping connections, so that he then possesses new faculties. Indeed, Lessing has said of himself that through a talent for critical observation, he had acquired for himself something that came near to genius. We have either to regard such abilities, founded on innate capacities, with wonder, or to consider them as fruits of experiences that the spirit self has had through the medium of a soul. They have been graven on this spirit self, and since they have not been implanted in this life, they must have been in a former one. The human spirit is its own species. Just as man as a physical being belonging to a species bequeaths his qualities within the species, so does the spirit bequeath its qualities within its species, that is, within itself. *In each life the human spirit appears as a repetition of itself with the fruits of its former experiences in previous lives.* This life is consequently the repetition of others and brings with it what the spirit self has, by work, acquired for itself in the previous life. When the spirit self absorbs something that can develop into fruit, it permeates itself with the life spirit. Just as the life body reproduces the form from species to species, so does the life spirit reproduce the soul from personal existence to personal existence.

Through the preceding considerations the thought that seeks the reason for certain life processes of man in repeated earth lives is raised into the sphere of validity. This idea can receive its full significance only by means of observations that spring from spiritual insight as it is acquired by following the path of knowledge described at the close of this book. Here it was only intended to show that ordinary observation rightly oriented by thinking already leads to this idea. Observation of this kind, it is true, will at first perceive the idea something like a silhouette, and it will not be possible to defend the idea entirely against the objections advanced by observation that is neither accurate nor guided aright by thinking. On the other hand, it is true that anyone who acquires such an idea through ordinary thoughtful observation, makes himself ready for supersensible observation. To a certain extent, he develops something that, of necessity, he must possess prior to this supersensible observation, just as one must have eyes prior to observing through the senses. Anyone who objects that through the formation of such an idea he can readily suggest to himself the supersensible observation proves only that he is incapable of entering into reality by means of free thinking and that it is just he who thus suggests to himself his own objections.

* * *

The experiences of the soul become lasting not only within the boundaries of birth and death, but beyond death. The soul, however, does not stamp its experiences

60

only on the spirit that flashes up within it. It impresses them, as has been shown, on the outer world also through its deeds. What a man did yesterday is today still present in its effects. A picture of the connection between cause and effect is given in the simile of sleep and death. Sleep has often been called the younger brother of death. I get up in the morning. My consecutive activity has been interrupted by the night. Now, under ordinary circumstances it is not possible for me to begin my activity again just as I please. I must connect it with my doings of yesterday if there is to be order and coherence in my life. My actions of yesterday are the conditions predetermining those actions that fall to me today. I have created my destiny of today by what I did yesterday. I have separated myself for awhile from my activity, but this activity belongs to me and draws me again to itself after I have withdrawn myself from it for awhile. My past remains bound up with me; it lives on in my present and will follow me into my future. If the effects of my deeds of yesterday were not to be my destiny of today, I should not have had to awake this morning, but to be newly created out of nothing. In the same way it would be absurd if under ordinary circumstances I were not to occupy a house that I have had built for me.

The human spirit is no more created anew when it begins its earthly life than a man is newly created every morning. Let us try to make clear to ourselves what happens when entrance into this life takes place. A physical body, receiving its form through the laws of heredity, makes its appearance. This body becomes the bearer of a spirit that repeats a previous life in a new form. Between the two stands the soul that leads a self-contained life of its own. Its inclinations and disinclinations, wishes and desires, minister to it. It presses thought into its service. As sentient soul, it receives the impressions of the outer world and carries them to the spirit in order that the spirit may extract from them the fruits that are permanent. It plays, as it were, the part of intermediary, and its task is fulfilled when it is adequate to this part. The body forms impressions for the sentient soul that transforms them into sensations, retains them in the memory as thought images, and surrenders them to the spirit to hold throughout duration. The soul is really that part of a man through which he belongs to his earthly life. Through his body he belongs to the physical human species; through it he is a member of this species. With his spirit he lives in a higher world. The soul binds the two worlds together for a time.

The physical world into which the human spirit enters, however, is no strange field of action to it. On it the traces of the spirit's actions are imprinted. Something in this field of action belongs to the spirit. It bears the impress of, and is related to, the spirit's being. Just as the soul formerly transmitted the impressions from the outer world to the spirit in order that they might become enduring in it, so now the soul, as the spirit's organ, has converted the capacities bestowed upon it by the spirit into deeds that are also enduring in their effects. Thus the soul has actually flowed into these actions. In the effects of his actions, a man's soul lives a second independent life. This statement provides us with a motive for examining life in order to see how the processes of destiny enter into it. Something happens to a man. He is probably at first inclined to regard such a happening as something coming into his life by chance, but he can become aware of how he himself is the outcome of such chances. Anyone who studies himself in his fortieth year, and in the search for his soul nature refuses to be content with an unreal, abstract conception of the "I," may well say to himself, "I am, indeed, nothing more nor less than what I have become through life's experiences, through what has happened to me by reason of destiny up to the present. Would I not be a different man today had I, for example, gone through a set of experiences different from those through which I actually went when I was twenty years of age?" The man will then seek his "I" not only in those impulses of development that come to him from within outwards, but also in what has formatively thrust itself into his life from without. He will recognize his own "I" in what happens to him. If we give ourselves up unreservedly to such a perception, then only one more really intimate observation of life is needed to show us that in what comes to us through certain experiences of destiny there is something that lays hold on the ego from without, just as memory, working from within, lays hold

63

on us in order to make a past experience flash up again. Thus we can make ourselves fitted to perceive in the experiences of destiny, how a former action of the soul finds its way to the ego, just as in memory an earlier experience, if called forth by an external cause, finds its way into the mind as a thought.

It has already been alluded to as a possible subject of consideration that the consequences of a deed may meet the human soul again. Regarding the consequences of some deeds, such a meeting is out of the question in the course of one earth life because that earth life was arranged especially for the carrying out of the deed. Experience lies in its fulfillment. In that case, a definite consequence of that action can no more re-act upon the soul than can someone remember an experience while still in the midst of it. It can only be a question here of the experience of the results of actions that do not meet the ego while it has the same disposition it had during the earth life in which the deed was done. Our gaze can only be directed to the consequences of action from another earth life. If an experience of destiny "befalls" us, and we feel that it is connected with the ego like something that has fashioned itself out of the ego's inner nature, then we can only think we have to do with the consequences of the actions of former earth lives. We see that we are led through an intimate thoughtful comprehension of life to the supposition—paradoxical to ordinary consciousness— that the experiences of destiny of one earth life are connected with the deeds of previous earth lives. This idea again can only receive its full content through supersensible knowledge; lacking this, it remains like a mere silhouette. Once more, however, this thought, this idea, gained by ordinary consciousness, prepares the soul so that it is enabled to behold its truth in actual supersensible observation.

Only one part of my deed is in the outer world; the other is in myself. Let us make this relation of the ego to the deed clear by a simple example from natural science. Animals that once could see migrated to the caves of Kentucky and, as a result of their life there, lost their power of sight. Existence in darkness deprived the eyes of their function. Consequently today the physical and chemical activity that normally occurs when seeing takes place is no longer carried on in these eyes. The stream of nourishment formerly expended on this activity now flows to other organs. These animals are now able to live only in these caves. They have by their act, by their immigration, created the conditions of their later life. The immigration has become a part of their destiny. A being that once acted has united itself with the results of its action. This is also true of the human spirit. The soul was only able to impart certain capacities to the spirit by performing actions, and these capacities correspond to the actions. Through an action that the soul has performed, there lives in the soul the energetic predisposition to perform another action that is the fruit of the first action.

The soul carries this as a necessity within itself until the subsequent action has taken place. One might also say that *through an action there has been imprinted upon the soul the necessity of carrying out the consequences of that action.*

By means of its actions the human spirit has really brought about its own destiny. In a new life it finds itself linked to what it did in a former one. It may be asked, "How can that be, when the human spirit on reincarnating finds itself in an entirely different world from the one it left at an earlier time?" This question is based on a superficial notion of the connections of destiny. If I change my scene of action from Europe to America, I also find myself in entirely new surroundings. Nevertheless, my life in America depends entirely on my previous life in Europe. If I have been a mechanic in Europe, my life in America will shape itself in quite a different way from what would have been the case had I been a bank clerk. In the one instance, I should probably be surrounded in America by machinery, in the other, by banking paraphernalia. In each case my previous life decides my environment. It attracts to itself, as it were, out of the whole surrounding world, those things that are related to it. So it is with the spirit self. It inevitably surrounds itself in a new life with what it is related to from previous lives. On that account sleep is an apt image of death because a man during sleep is withdrawn from the field of action in which his destiny awaits him. While we sleep, events in this field of action pursue their course. We have for a certain time no influence on this course of events. Our life on a new day depends, nevertheless, on the effects of the deeds of the previous day. Our personality actually embodies or incarnates itself anew every morning in our world of action. What was separated from us during the night is spread out around us, as it were, during the day. So it is with the actions of former human embodiments or incarnations. They are bound up with a man as his destiny, just as life in the dark Kentucky caves remains bound up with the animals that, by migrating into them, have lost their power of sight. Just as these animals can only live in the surroundings in which they have placed themselves, so the human spirit is able to live only in the surroundings that it has created for itself by its acts. That I find in the morning a certain state of affairs, created by me on the previous day, is brought about by the immediate course of events. That I find surroundings when I reincarnate corresponding to the results of my deeds in a previous life, is brought about by the relationship of my reincarnated spirit with the things in the surrounding world. From this we can form an idea of how the soul is set into the human constitution. The physical body is subject to the laws of heredity. The human spirit, on the contrary, has to incarnate over and over again, and its law consists in its bringing over the fruits of the former lives into the following ones. The soul lives in the present, but this life in the present is not independent of the previous lives be-

67

cause the incarnating spirit brings its destiny with it from its previous incarnations. This destiny determines life. What impressions the soul will be able to have, what wishes it will be able to have gratified, what sorrows and joys shall develop for it, with what men and women it shall come into contact—all this depends upon the nature of the actions in the past incarnations of the spirit. The soul must meet those people again in a subsequent life with whom it was bound up in a previous life because the actions that have taken place between them must have their consequences. When this soul seeks re-embodiment, those other souls that are bound up with it will also strive towards their incarnation at the same time. The life of the soul is, therefore, the result of the self-created destiny of the human spirit. The course of man's life between birth and death is determined in a threefold way. In consequence, he is dependent in a threefold way on factors that lie on the other side of birth and death. The body is subject to the law of heredity; the soul is subject to its self-created destiny. We call this destiny, created by man himself, his *karma*. The spirit is under the law of *re-embodiment,* repeated earth lives. One can accordingly also express the relationship between spirit, soul and body in the following way. The spirit is immortal; birth and death reign over the body according to the laws of the physical world; the soul life, which is subject to destiny, mediates the connection of both during an earthly life. All further knowledge about the being of man presupposes acquaintance with the three worlds to which he belongs. These three worlds are dealt with in the following pages.

Thinking that frankly faces the phenomena of life and is not afraid to follow out to their final consequences the thoughts resulting from a living, vivid contemplation of life can, by pure logic, arrive at the conception of the law of karma and repeated incarnations. Just as it is true that for the seer with the opened spiritual eye, past lives lie like an open book before him as experience, so it is true that the truth of these things can become obvious to the unbiased reason that reflects upon it.

What is said here should be compared with the *Addenda* at the end of the book.

Chapter III

THE THREE WORLDS

1. The Soul World

OUR study of man has shown that he belongs to three worlds. The materials and forces that build up his body are taken from the world of physical bodies. He has knowledge of this world through the perceptions of his outer physical senses. Anyone trusting to these senses alone and developing only their perceptive capacities can gain no enlightenment for himself concerning the two other worlds, the soul world and the world of the spirit. A man's ability to convince himself of the reality of a thing or a being depends on whether he has an organ of perception, a sense for it. It may, of course, easily lead to misunderstanding if we call the higher organs of perception spiritual senses as is done here because in speaking of senses we involuntarily connect the thought of the physical with them. The physical world is, in fact, designated the sensory, in contradistinction to the *spirit-*

ual. In order to avoid this misunderstanding, we must take into account the fact that higher senses are spoken of here only in a comparative or metaphorical sense. Just as the physical senses perceive the physical, so do the soul and spiritual senses perceive the soul and spiritual worlds. The expression, sense, will be used as meaning simply organ of perception. A man would have no knowledge of light and color had he no eye sensitive to light; he would know nothing of sound had he no ear sensitive to sound. In this connection the German philosopher, Lotze, says rightly, "Without a light-sensitive eye and a sound-sensitive ear, the whole world would be dark and silent. There would be in it just as little light or sound as there could be toothache without the pain-sensitive nerve of the tooth."

In order to see what is said here in the proper way, one need only think how entirely differently the world must reveal itself to man from the way it does to the lower forms of animal life that have only a kind of sense of touch or feeling spread over the whole surface of their bodies. Light, color and sound certainly cannot exist for them in the same way they do for beings gifted with ears and eyes. The vibrations caused by the firing of a gun may have an effect on them also if, as a result, sensitive areas are excited, but in order that these vibrations of the air exhibit themselves to the soul as a shot, an ear is necessary. An eye is necessary in order that certain processes in the fine matter called ether reveal themselves as light

71

and color. We only know something about a being or thing because we are affected by it through one of our organs.

This relationship of man with the world of realities is brought out extremely well by Goethe when he says, "It is really in vain that we try to express the nature of a thing. We become aware of effects and a complete history of these effects would indeed embrace the nature of that thing. We endeavor in vain to describe the character of a man. If instead we put together his actions and deeds, a picture of his character will present itself to us. Colors are the deeds of light—deeds and sufferings. . . . Colors and light are, to be sure, linked in the most precise relationship, but we must think of them both as belonging to the whole of nature, because through them the whole of nature is engaged in revealing itself especially to the eye. In like manner, nature reveals itself to another sense. . . . Nature thus speaks downwards to the other senses— to known, unknown, and unrecognized senses. It thus speaks to itself and to us through a thousand phenomena. To the attentive, nature is nowhere either dead or silent."

It would not be correct were one to interpret this saying of Goethe as though the possibility of knowing the essential nature of things were denied by it. Goethe does not mean that we perceive only the effects of a thing, and that the being thereof hides itself behind them. He means rather that one should not speak at all of a "hidden being." The being is not behind its manifestation. On the contrary, it comes into view through the manifestation. This being, however, is in many respects so rich that it can manifest itself to other senses in still other forms. What reveals itself does belong to the being, but because of the limitations of the senses, it is not the whole being. This thought of Goethe corresponds entirely with the views of spiritual science set forth here.

Just as in the body, eye and ear develop as organs of perception, as senses for bodily processes, so does a man develop in himself soul and spiritual organs of perception through which the soul and spiritual worlds are opened to him. For those who do not have such higher senses, these worlds are dark and silent, just as the bodily world is dark and silent for a being without eyes and ears. It is true that the relation of man to these higher senses is rather different from his relation to the bodily senses. It is good Mother Nature who sees to it, as a rule, that these latter are fully developed in him. They come into existence without his help. For the development of his higher senses, however, he must work himself. If he wishes to perceive the soul and spirit worlds, he must develop soul and spirit, just as nature has developed his body so that he might perceive the corporeal world around him and guide himself in it. Such a development of the higher organs not yet developed for us by nature itself is not unnatural because in the higher sense all that man accomplishes belongs also to nature.

Only the person who is ready to maintain that man

should remain standing at the stage at which he left the hand of nature, could call the development of the higher senses unnatural. By him the significances of these organs is misunderstood, "unrecognized," as indicated in the quotation of Goethe. Such a person might just as well oppose all human education because it also develops further the work of nature. He would also have to oppose operations upon those born blind, because almost the same thing that happens to the person born blind when operated upon happens to the man who awakens the higher sense in himself in the manner set forth in the last part of this book. The world appears to him with new qualities, events and facts, about which the physical senses reveal nothing. It is clear to him that through these higher organs he adds nothing arbitrarily to reality, but that without them the essential part of this reality would have remained hidden from him. The soul and spirit worlds are not to be thought of as being alongside or outside the physical world. They are not separated in space from it. Just as for persons born blind and operated upon, the previously dark world flashes out in light and colors, so do things that previously were only corporeal phenomena reveal their soul and spirit qualities to anyone who is awakened in soul and spirit. It is true, moreover, that this world then becomes filled with other occurrences and beings that remain completely unknown to those whose soul and spirit senses are unawakened. (The development of the soul and spirit senses will be spoken of in a more

74

detailed way farther on in this book. Here these higher worlds themselves will be first described. Anyone who denies their existence says nothing more than that he has not yet developed his higher organs. The evolution of humanity is not terminated at any one stage; it must always progress.)

The higher organs are often involuntarily pictured as too similar to the physical organs. It should be understood that these organs are spiritual or soul formations. It ought not to be expected, therefore, that what is perceived in the higher worlds should be only something like a cloudy, attenuated form of matter. As long as something is expected of this kind, no clear idea can be formed of what is really meant here by higher worlds. For many persons it would not be nearly as difficult as it actually is to know something about these higher worlds—of course, at first only about the elementary regions—if they did not form the idea that what they are to see is again merely rarefied physical matter. Since they take for granted something of this kind, they are not at all willing, as a rule, to recognize what they are really dealing with. They look upon it as unreal, and refuse to acknowledge it as something satisfactory. True, the higher stages of spiritual development are accessible only with difficulty. Those stages, however, that suffice for the perception of the nature of the spiritual world—and that is already a great deal—should not be at all difficult to reach if people would first free themselves from the misconception that consists in picturing to themselves the soul and spiritual merely as a finer physical.

Just as we do not know a man entirely when we have only visualized his physical exterior, so also do we not know the world around us if we only know what the physical senses reveal to us about it. Just as a photograph grows intelligible and living to us when we have become so intimately acquainted with the person photographed that we know his soul, so can we really understand the corporeal world only when we gain a knowledge of its soul and spiritual basis. For this reason it is advisable to speak here first about the higher worlds, the worlds of soul and spirit, and only then judge the physical from the viewpoint of spiritual science.

At this present stage of civilization certain difficulties are encountered by anyone speaking about the higher worlds because this age is great above all things in its knowledge and conquest of the physical world. Our words have, in fact, received their stamp and significance in relation to this physical world. We must, nevertheless, make use of these current words in order to form a link with something known. This, however, opens the door to many misunderstandings on the part of those who are willing to trust only their external senses. Much can at first be expressed and indicated only by means of similes and comparisons. This must be so, for such similes are a means by which the seeker is at first directed to these higher worlds, and through which his own ascent to them is furthered. Of this ascent I shall speak in a later chapter, in which the development of the soul and spiritual organs of perception will be dealt with.* To begin with, man must gain knowledge of the higher worlds by means of similes. Only then is he ready to acquire for himself the power to see into them.

Just as the matter and forces that compose and govern our stomach, heart, brain, lungs, and so forth, come from the physical world, so do our soul qualities, our impulses, desires, feelings, passions, wishes and sensations, come from the soul world. The soul of man is a member of this soul world, just as his body is part of the world of physical bodies. If we want at the outset to indicate a difference between the corporeal and soul worlds, we could say that the soul world is in all objects and entities much finer, more mobile and plastic than the former. It must be kept clearly in mind, however, that on entering the soul world we enter a world entirely different from the physical. If, therefore, the words "coarser" and "finer" are used in this respect, readers must be fully aware that something is suggested by way of comparison that is, nevertheless, actually fundamentally different. This is true in regard to all that is said about the soul world in words borrowed from the world of physical corporeality. Taking this into account, we can say that the formations and beings of the soul world consist in the same way of soul substances, and are directed by soul forces in much the same way as is the

* See *Addendum 8.*

case in the physical world with physical substances and physical forces.

Just as spatial extension and spatial movement are peculiar to corporeal formations, so are excitability and impelling desire peculiar to the things and beings of the soul world. For this reason the soul world is described as the world of desires or wishes, or as the world of longing. These expressions are borrowed from the human soul world. We must, therefore, hold fast to the idea that the things in those parts of the soul world that lie outside the human soul are just as different from the soul forces within it as the physical matter and forces of the external corporeal world are different from those parts that compose the physical human body. Impulse, wish, longing, are names for the substantiality of the soul world. To this substantiality let us give the name *astral*. If we pay more attention specifically to the forces of the soul world, we can speak of *desire-being,* but it must not be forgotten that the distinction between substance and force cannot be as sharply drawn as in the physical world. An impulse can just as well be called force as substance.

The differences between the soul world and the physical have a bewildering effect on anyone who obtains a view of the soul world for the first time, but that is also the case when a previously inactive physical sense is opened. The man born blind has first to learn after an operation how to guide himself through the world he has previously known only by means of the sense of touch. Such a person, for

78

example, sees the objects at first in his eyes, then outside himself, but they appear to him as though painted on a flat surface. Only gradually does he grasp perspective and the spatial distance between things. In the soul world entirely different laws prevail from those in the physical. To be sure, many soul formations are bound to those of the other worlds. The human soul, for instance, is bound to the human body and to the human spirit. The occurrences we can observe in it are, therefore, influenced at the same time by the corporeal and spiritual worlds. We have to take this into account in observing the soul world, and we must take care not to claim as a law of the soul world occurrences due to the influence of another world. When, for example, a man sends out a wish, that wish is brought to birth by a thought, by a conception of the spirit whose laws it accordingly follows. Just as we can formulate the laws of the physical world by disregarding, for example, the influence of man on its processes, so the same thing is possible with regard to the soul world.

An important difference between soul and physical processes can be expressed by saying that the reciprocal action in the processes of the soul is much more inward than in the physical. In physical space there reigns, for example, the law of impact. When an ivory ball strikes a ball at rest, the resting ball will move in a direction that can be calculated from the motion and elasticity of the first. In soul space the reciprocal action of two forms that encounter each other depends on their inner qualities. If they are in affinity they mutually interpenetrate and, as it were, grow together. They repel each other if their natures are in conflict. In physical space there are also definite laws of vision. We see distant objects perspectively diminishing. When we look down an avenue, the distant trees appear, according to the laws of perspective, to stand closer together than those nearby. In the soul space, on the contrary, all objects near or far appear to the clairvoyant at distances apart that are in accordance with their inner nature. This is naturally a source of the most manifold errors for those who enter the soul world and wish to be at home there with the help of the rules they bring from the physical world.

One of the first things a man must acquire in order to make his way about the soul world is the ability to distinguish the various kinds of forms found there in much the same way he distinguishes solid, liquid, air or gaseous bodies in the physical world. In order to do this, he must know the two most important basic forces to be found in the soul world. They may be called *sympathy* and *antipathy*. The nature of any soul formation is determined according to the way these basic forces operate in it. The force with which one soul formation attracts others, seeks to fuse with them and to make its affinity with them effective, must be designated as *sympathy*. *Antipathy* is the force with which soul formations repel, exclude each other in the soul world. It is the force with which they assert their separate identities. The part played by a soul

80

formation in the soul world depends upon the proportion in which these basic forces are present in it. In the first place, we must distinguish three kinds of soul formations that are determined by the way sympathy and antipathy work in them. That these formations differ from each other is due to the fact that sympathy and antipathy have in them definitely fixed mutual relationships. In all three both basic forces are present.

To begin with, let us consider the first of these soul formations. It attracts other formations in its neighborhood by means of the sympathy ruling in it. Besides this sympathy, there is at the same time antipathy present by which it repels certain things in its surroundings. From the outside such a formation appears to be endowed only with the forces of antipathy. That, however, is not the case. Both sympathy and antipathy are present in it, but the latter predominates. It has the upper hand over the former. Such formations play a self-seeking role in soul space. They repel much that surrounds them, and lovingly attract but little to themselves. They therefore move through the soul space as unchangeable forms. The force of sympathy that they possess appears greedy. This greed appears at the same time insatiable, as if it could not be satisfied, because the predominating antipathy repels so much of what approaches that no satisfaction is possible. This kind of soul formation corresponds with the solid physical bodies of the physical world. This region of soul matter may be called *Burning Desire*. The part of Burning

Desire that is mingled with the souls of animals and men determines in them what we call their lower sensual impulses, their dominating selfish instincts.

In the second kind of soul formations the two basic forces preserve a balance. Accordingly, antipathy and sympathy act in them with equal strength. They aproach other formations with a certain neutrality. They act on them as though related, but without especially attracting or repelling. They erect, as it were, no solid barrier between themselves and their surroundings. They constantly allow other formations in their surroundings to act on them. We can, therefore, compare them with the liquids of the physical world. There is nothing of greed in the way such formations attract others to themselves. The activity meant here may be recognized, for example, when the human soul receives the sensation of a certain color. If I have the sensation of a red color, I receive, to begin with, a neutral stimulus from my surroundings. Only when pleasure in the red color is added to this stimulus does another soul activity come into play. What effects the neutral stimulus is the action of soul formations standing in such reciprocal relationship that sympathy and antipathy preserve an equal balance. The soul substance considered here must be described as a perfectly plastic and mobile substance. It does not move through soul space in a self-seeking way like the first, but by such means that its being receives impressions everywhere, and shows itself to have affinity with much that approaches it.

82

An expression that might be applied to it is *Mobile Sensitivity*.

The third variety of soul formations is that in which sympathy has the upper hand over antipathy. Antipathy produces self-seeking self-assertion. This, however, retires into the background when inclination towards the things in the surrounding world takes its place. Let us picture such a formation within the soul space. It appears as the center of an attracting sphere that spreads over the objects surrounding it. Such formations must be specially designated as *Wish Substance*. This designation appears to be the right one because through the existing antipathy, although relatively weaker than the sympathy, the attraction works in such a way that it endeavors to bring the attracted objects within the soul formation's own sphere. The sympathy thus receives an underlying tone of selfishness. This wish substance may be likened to the air or gaseous bodies of the physical world. Just as a gas strives to expand on all sides, so does the wish substance spread itself out in all directions.

Higher levels of soul substance characterize themselves in that one of the basic forces, antipathy, retires completely into the background and sympathy alone shows itself to be really effective. Now this sympathy is able to make its power felt primarily within the various parts of the soul formation itself. These parts act with reciprocal attraction upon each other. The force of sympathy within a soul formation comes to expression in what one calls *Liking,* and each lessening of this sympathy is *Disliking.* Disliking is only lessened liking, as cold is only a lessened warmth. Liking and disliking is what lives in man as the world of feelings in the more restricted sense of the word. Feeling is the life and activity of the soul within itself. What is called the *comfort* of the soul depends on the way the feelings of liking and disliking, attraction and repulsion, interact within the soul.

A still higher stage is represented by those soul formations in which sympathy does not remain shut up within the region of their own life. They, and also the fourth stage, differ from the three lower stages by virtue of the fact that in them the force of sympathy has no antipathy opposing it to overcome. It is only through these higher orders of soul substance that the manifold variety of soul formations can unite and form a common soul world. To the degree that antipathy comes into play, the soul formation strives toward some other thing for the sake of its own life, and in order to strengthen and enrich itself by means of the other. Where antipathy is inactive, the other thing is received as revelation, as information. This higher form of soul substance plays a similar role in the soul space to that played by light in physical space. It causes one soul formation to suck in, as it were, the being or essence of others for their own sakes; one could also say, to let itself be shone upon by them. Only by drawing upon these higher regions are the soul beings awakened to the true soul life. Their dull life in the darkness opens outwards and begins to shine and ray out into soul space. The sluggish, dull weaving within itself that seeks to shut itself off through antipathy when the substances of the lower regions alone are present, becomes force and mobility that goes forth from within and pours itself outwards in streams. The Mobile Sensitivity of the second region is only effective when formations meet each other. Then, indeed, the one streams over into the other, but contact is here necessary. In the higher regions there prevails a free out-raying and out-pouring. The essential nature of this region is quite rightly described as an "outraying," because the sympathy that is developed acts in such a way that this expression, taken from the action of light, can be used as a symbol for it. Just as plants degenerate in a dark cellar, so do the soul formations degenerate without the life-giving soul substances of the higher regions. *Soul Light, Active Soul Force* and the true *Soul Life* in the narrower sense, belong to these regions and thence pour themselves into the soul beings.

Thus one has to distinguish between three lower and three higher regions of the soul world. These two are linked together by a fourth, so that there results the following division of the soul world.

1. Region of Burning Desire
2. Region of Mobile Sensitivity
3. Region of Wishes
4. Region of Liking and Disliking

85

5. Region of Soul Light
6. Region of Active Soul Force
7. Region of Soul Life

Throughout the first three regions, the soul formations receive their qualities from the relative proportions of sympathy and antipathy. Throughout the fourth region sympathy weaves its web within the soul formations themselves. Throughout the three highest, the power of sympathy becomes ever more free. Illumining and quickening, the soul substances of this region flow through the soul space, awakening what, if left to itself, would lose itself in its own separate existence.

Though it should be superfluous, for the sake of clarity it must be emphasized that these seven divisions of the soul world do not represent regions separated one from another. Just as in the physical world, solid, liquid and air or gaseous substances interpenetrate, so in the soul world do Burning Desire, Mobile Sensitivity and the forces of the World of Wishes. Just as in the physical world warmth penetrates bodies and light illumines them, so it is also the case in the soul world with Liking and Disliking, and with the Soul Light. Something similar takes place with regard to the Active Soul Force and the true Soul Life.

2. *The Soul in the Soul World after Death*

The soul is the connecting link between the spirit of man and his body. Its forces of sympathy and antipathy that, owing to their mutual relationship, bring about soul manifestations such as desire, sensitivity, wish, liking and aversion, and so forth, are not only active between soul formation and soul formation, but they manifest themselves also in relation to the beings of the other worlds, the physical and the spiritual. While the soul lives in the body, it participates, so to speak, in all that takes place in the body. When the physical functions of the body proceed with regularity, pleasure and comfort arise in the soul. If these functions are disturbed, discomfort and pain arise. The soul, however, has its share in the activities of the spirit also. One thought fills it with joy, another with abhorrence; a correct judgment has the approval of the soul, a false one its disapproval. The stage of evolution of a man depends, in fact, on whether the inclinations of his soul move more in one direction or in another. A man is the more perfect, the more his soul sympathizes with the manifestations of the spirit. He is the more imperfect the more the inclinations of his soul are satisfied by the functions of his body.

The spirit is the central point of man, the body the intermediary by which the spirit observes and learns to understand the physical world, and through which it acts in that world. The soul is the intermediary between the two.

It liberates the sensation of sound from the physical impression that the vibrations of the air make on the ear. It experiences pleasure in this sound. All this it communicates to the spirit, which thereby attains to the understanding of the physical world. A thought, which arises in the spirit, is transformed by the soul into the wish to realize it, and only through this can the thought become a deed with the help of the body as an instrument. Now man can fulfill his destiny only by allowing his spirit to direct the course of all his activity. The soul can by its own power direct its inclinations just as readily to the physical as to the spiritual. It sends, as it were, its feelers down into the physical as well as up into the spiritual. By sinking them into the physical world, the soul's own being becomes saturated and colored by the nature of the physical. Since the spirit is able to act in the physical world only through the soul as intermediary, this spirit itself is thus given the direction towards the physical. Its formations are drawn toward the physical by the forces of the soul. Observe, for example, the undeveloped human being. The inclinations of his soul cling to the functions of his body. He feels pleasure only in the impressions made by the physical world on his senses. His intellectual life also is thereby completely drawn down into this region. His thoughts serve only to satisfy his physical needs. Since the spiritual self lives from incarnation to incarnation, it is intended to receive its direction ever increasingly from the spiritual. Its knowledge should be determined by the spirit of eternal truth; its action by eternal goodness.

Death, regarded as a fact in the physical world, signifies a change in the functions of the body. At death the body ceases to function as the intermediary between the soul and the spirit. In its processes it shows itself henceforth entirely subject to the physical world and its laws, and it passes over into it in order to dissolve therein. Only these physical processes of the body can be observed after death by the physical senses. What happens to the soul and spirit, however, escapes these senses because even during life, soul and spirit cannot be observed by the senses except insofar as they attain to external expression in physical processes. After death this kind of expression is no longer possible. For this reason, observation by means of the physical senses and the science based on it does not come under consideration in reference to the fate of the soul and spirit after death. Here a higher knowledge steps in that is based on observation of what takes place in the soul and spirit worlds.

After the spirit has released itself from the body, it still continues to be united with the soul. Just as during physical life the body chained it to the physical world, so now the soul chains the spirit to the soul world. It is not in this soul world, however, that the spirit's true, primordial being is to be found. The soul world is intended to serve merely as its connecting link with the scene of its actions, the physical world. In order to appear in a new incarnation with a more perfect form, the spirit must draw force and renewed strength from the spiritual world. Through the soul it has become entangled in the physical world. It is bound to a soul being, which is saturated and colored by the nature of the physical, and through this has acquired a tendency in that direction. After death the soul is no longer bound to the body, but only to the spirit. It lives now within soul surroundings. Only the forces of this soul world can, therefore, have an effect on it. At first the spirit also is bound to this life of the soul in the soul world. It is bound to it in the same way it is bound to the body during physical incarnation. When the body shall die is determined by the laws of the body. Speaking generally, it must be said that it is not the soul and spirit that forsake the body, but they are set free by the body when its forces are no longer able to fulfill the purpose of the human organism.

The relationship between soul and spirit is just the same. The soul will set the spirit free to pass into the higher, spiritual world, when its forces are no longer able to fulfill the purpose of the human soul organism. The spirit is set free the moment the soul has handed over to dissolution what it can experience only in the body, retaining only what can live on with the spirit. This remainder, although experienced in the body, can nevertheless be impressed on the spirit as fruit. It connects the soul with the spirit in the purely spiritual world. In order to learn the fate of the soul after death, the process of dissolution must be observed. It had the task of giving the spirit its direction toward the physical. The moment it has fulfilled this task, the soul takes the direction toward the spiritual. In fact, the nature of its task would cause it henceforth to be only spiritually active when the body falls away from it, that is, when it can no longer be a connecting link. So it would be, had it not, owing to its life in the body, been influenced by the body and in its inclinations been attracted to it. Without this coloring received through the body, it would at once on being disembodied follow the laws of the spirit-soul world only and manifest no further inclination toward the sense world. This would be the case if a man on dying lost completely all interest in the earthly world, if all desires and wishes attaching him to the existence he has left had been completely satisfied. To the extent that this is not the case, all that remains of his interest clings to the soul.

To avoid confusion we must carefully distinguish here between what chains man to the world in such a way that it can be adjusted in a subsequent incarnation, and what chains him to one particular incarnation, that is, to the one just passed. The first is made good by means of the law of destiny, karma. The second can only be got rid of by the soul after death.

After death there follows for the human spirit a time during which the soul is shaking off its inclinations toward physical existence in order to follow once more the laws of the spirit-soul world only and thus set the spirit free. The more the soul was bound to the physical, the longer, naturally, will this time last. It will be short for the man who has clung but little to physical life, and long for one whose interests are completely bound up with it, who at death has many desires, wishes and impulses still living in the soul.

The easiest way to gain an idea of the condition in which the soul lives during the time immediately after death is afforded by the following consideration. Let us take a somewhat crass example—the pleasure of the *bon vivant*. His pleasure is derived from food. The pleasure is naturally not bodily but belongs to the soul. The pleasure lives in the soul as does the desire for the pleasure. To satisfy the desire, however, the corresponding bodily organs, the palate, etc., are necessary. After death the soul has not immediately lost such a desire, but it no longer possesses the bodily organ that provides the means for satisfying it. For another reason, but one that acts far more strongly in the same way, the human soul now experiences all the suffering of burning thirst that one would undergo in a waterless waste. The soul thus suffers burning pain by being deprived of the pleasure because it has laid aside the bodily organ through which it can experience that pleasure. It is the same with all that the soul yearns for and that can only be satisfied through the bodily organs. This condition of burning privation lasts until the soul has learned to cease longing for what can only be satisfied through the body. The time passed in this condition may be called the region of desires, although it has of course nothing to do with a "locality."

When the soul enters the soul world after death it becomes subject to the laws of that world. The laws act on it and the manner in which the soul's inclinations towards the physical are destroyed depends upon their action. The way these laws act on the soul must differ depending upon the kinds of soul substances and soul forces in whose domain it is placed at the time. Each of these according to its kind will make its purifying, cleansing influence felt. The process that takes place here is such that all antipathy in the soul is gradually overcome by the forces of sympathy. This sympathy itself is brought to its highest pitch because, through this highest degree of sympathy with the rest of the soul world, the soul will, as it were, merge into and become one with it. Then will it be utterly emptied of self-seeking. It ceases to exist as a being inclined to physically sensible existence, and the spirit is set free by it. The soul, therefore, purifies itself through all the regions of the soul world described above until, in the region of perfect sympathy, it becomes one with the general soul world. That the spirit itself is in bondage until this last moment of the liberation of its soul is due to the fact that through its life the spirit has become most intimately related to the soul. This relationship is much closer than the one with the body because the spirit is only indirectly bound to the body through the soul, whereas it is bound directly to the soul. The soul is, in fact, the

93

spirit's own life. For this reason the spirit is not bound to the decaying body, although it is bound to the soul that is gradually freeing itself. On account of the immediate bond between the spirit and the soul, the spirit can feel free of the soul only when the soul has itself become one with the general soul world.

To the extent the soul world is the abode of man immediately after death, it is called the *region of desires*. The various religious systems that have embodied in their doctrines a knowledge of these conditions are acquainted with this region of desire under the name "purgatory," "cleansing fire," and the like.

The *lowest region* of the soul world is that of Burning Desire. Everything in the soul that has to do with the coarsest, lowest, most selfish desires of the physical life is purged from the soul after death by it, because through such desires it is exposed to the effects of the forces of this soul region. The unsatisfied desires that have remained over from physical life furnish the points of attack. The sympathy of such souls only extends to what can nourish their selfish natures. It is greatly exceeded by the antipathy that floods everything else. Now the desires aim at physical enjoyments that cannot be satisfied in the soul world. The craving is intensified to the highest degree by the impossibility of satisfaction. Owing to this impossibility, at the same time it is forced to die out gradually. The burning lusts gradually exhaust themselves and the soul learns by experience that the only means of

94

preventing the suffering that must come from such longings lies in extirpating them. During physical life satisfaction is ever and again attained. By this means the pain of the burning lusts is covered over by a kind of illusion. After death in the "cleansing fire" the pain comes into evidence quite unveiled. The corresponding experiences of privation are passed through. It is a dark, gloomy state indeed in which the soul thus finds itself. Of course, only those persons whose desires are directed during physical life to the coarsest things can fall into this condition. Natures with few lusts go through it without noticing it because they have no affinity with it. It must be stated that souls are the longer influenced by burning desire the more closely they have become related to that fire through their physical life. On that account there is more need for them to be purified in it. Such purification should not be described as suffering in the sense of this expression as it is used in the sense world. The soul after death *demand*s its purification since an existing imperfection can only thus be purged away.

In the *second region* of the soul world there are processes in which sympathy and antipathy preserve an equal balance. Insofar as a human soul is in that condition after death it will be influenced by what takes place in this region for a time. The losing of oneself in the external glitter of life, the joy in the swiftly succeeding impressions of the senses, bring about this condition. People live in it to the extent it is brought about by the soul inclinations

95

just indicated. They allow themselves to be influenced by each worthless trifle of everyday life, but since their sympathy is attached to no one thing in particular, the influences pass quickly. Everything that does not belong to this region of empty nothings is repellent to such persons. When the soul experiences this condition after death without the presence of the physical objects that are necessary for its satisfaction, the condition must ultimately die out. Naturally, the privation that precedes its complete extinction in the soul is full of suffering. This state of suffering is the school for the destruction of the illusion a man is wrapped up in during physical life.

Then a *third region* of the soul world is to be considered in which the phenomena of sympathy, of the wish nature, predominate. Souls experience the effects of these phenomena from everything that preserves an atmosphere of wishes after death. These wishes also gradually die out because of the impossibility of satisfying them.

The region of Liking and Disliking in the soul world that has been described above as the *fourth region* imposes special trials on the soul. As long as the soul dwells in the body it shares all that concerns the body. The inner surge of liking and disliking is bound up with the body. The body causes the soul's feeling of well-being and comfort, dislike and discomfort. During his physical life man feels that his body is himself. What is called the feeling of self is based upon this fact, and the more people are inclined to be sensuous, the more does their feeling of self take on this character. After death the body, the object of the feeling of self, is lacking. On this account the soul, which still retains such a feeling, has the sensation of being emptied out as it were. A feeling as if it had lost itself overcomes the soul. This continues until it has been recognized that the true human being does not lie in the physical. The impressions made by this fourth region on the soul accordingly destroy the illusion of the bodily self. The soul learns to feel this corporeality no longer as an essential reality. It is cured and purified of its attachment to the body. In this way it has conquered what previously chained it strongly to the physical world, and it can now unfold fully the forces of sympathy that flow outwards. It has, so to speak, broken free from itself and is ready to pour itself into the common soul world with full sympathy.

It should not pass unnoted that the experiences of this region are suffered to an especial degree by suicides. Such a one leaves his physical body in an artificial way, although all the feelings connected with it remain unchanged. In the case of natural death, the decay of the body is accompanied by a partial dying out of the feelings of attachment to it. In the case of suicides there are, in addition to the torment caused by the feeling of having been suddenly emptied out, the unsatisfied desires and wishes because of which they have deprived themselves of their bodies.

The *fifth stage* of the soul world is that of Soul Light. In it sympathy with others has already reached a high degree of importance. Souls are connected with this stage insofar as they did not lose themselves in the satisfaction of lower necessities during their physical lives, but had joy and pleasure in their surroundings. Over-enthusiasm for nature, for example, in that it has borne something of a sensuous character, undergoes purifying here. It is necessary, however, to distinguish clearly this kind of love of nature from the higher living in nature that is of the spiritual kind that seeks for the spirit revealing itself in the things and events of nature. This kind of feeling for nature is one of the things that develop the spirit itself and establishes something permanent in it! One must distinguish, however, between such a feeling for nature, and a pleasure in nature that is based on the senses. In regard to this, the soul requires purification just as well as in regard to other inclinations based on mere physical existence. Many people see a kind of ideal in the arrangements of civilization that serve sensuous well-being, and in a system of education that, above all, brings about sensuous comfort. One cannot say that they seek to further only their selfish impulses. Their souls are, nevertheless, directed toward the physical world and must be cured of this by the force of sympathy that rules in the fifth region of the soul world and lacks these external means of gratification. Here the soul gradually recognizes that this sympathy must take other directions. These are found in the outpouring of the soul into the soul region, which is brought about by sympathy with the soul surroundings.

Those souls also are purified here that mainly seek an enhancement of their sensuous welfare from their religious observances, whether it be that their longing goes out to an earthly or to a heavenly paradise. They, indeed, find this paradise in the "soul-land," but only for the purpose of seeing through its worthlessness. These are, of course, merely a few detached examples of purifications that take place in this fifth region. They could be multiplied indefinitely.

By means of the *sixth region,* that of Active Soul Force, the purification of the part of the soul that thirsts for action takes place in souls whose activity does not bear an egotistical character but springs, nevertheless, from the sensuous satisfaction that action affords them. Viewed superficially, natures that develop such a desire for action convey the impression of being idealists; they show themselves to be persons capable of self-sacrifice. In a deeper sense, however, the chief thing with them is the enhancement of a sensuous feeling of pleasure. Many artistic natures and those who give themselves up to scientific activity because it pleases them belong to this class. These people are bound to the physical world by the belief that art and science exist for the sake of such pleasure.

The *seventh region,* that of the real Soul Life, frees man from his last inclinations to the sensory physical world. Each preceding region takes up from the soul whatever has affinity with it. The part of the soul still enveloping the spirit is the belief that its activity should be entirely devoted to the physical world. There are highly gifted individuals whose thoughts, however, are occupied with scarcely anything but the occurrences of the physical world. This belief can be called materialistic. It must be destroyed, and this is done in the seventh region. There the souls see that in true reality there exist no objects for materialistic thinking. Like ice in the sun, this belief of the soul melts away. The soul being is now absorbed into its own world. Now free of all fetters the spirit rises to the regions where it lives entirely in surroundings of its own nature. The soul had completed its previous earthly task, and after death any traces of this task that remained fettering the spirit have dissolved. By overcoming the last trace of the earthly, the soul is itself given back to its own element.

One sees from this description that the experiences in the soul world, and also the conditions of soul life after death, take on an ever less repellent character the more a man has stripped off those elements adhering to him from his earthly union with the physical corporeality and that were directly related to his body. The soul will belong for a longer or shorter time to one or another region according to the conditions created during its physical life. Wherever the soul feels affinity, there it remains until the affinity is extinguished. Where no relation exists, it goes on its way without feeling the possible effects.

It was intended that only the fundamental characteristics of the soul world and the outstanding features of the life of the soul in this world should be described here. This applies also to the following descriptions of the spiritland. It would exceed the prescribed limits of this book were further descriptions of the characteristics of these higher worlds attempted. The spatial relationships and the time lapses—terms that can only be used by way of comparison because the conditions are quite different there from those obtaining in the physical world—can only be discussed intelligibly when one is prepared to deal with them adequately and in full detail. References of importance in this connection will be found in my *Occult Science, an Outline*.

3. The Spiritland

Before the spirit can be observed on its further pilgrimage, the region it enters must first be examined. It is the world of the spirit. This world is so unlike the physical that all that is said about it will appear fantastic to anyone who is only willing to trust his physical senses. What has already been said in regard to the world of the soul—that is, that we have to use analogies to describe it—also holds good here to a still higher degree. Our language, which for the most part serves only for the realities of the senses, is not richly blessed with expressions applicable directly to the spiritland. It is, therefore, especially necessary to ask the reader to understand much that is said as an indication only because everything that is described here is so unlike the physical world that only in this way can it be depicted. The author is ever conscious of how little this account can really resemble the experiences of this region owing to the imperfection of our language, calculated as it is to be our medium of expression for the physical world.

It must above all things be emphasized that this world is woven out of the substance of which human thought consists. The word "substance," too, is here used in a far from strict or accurate sense. Thought, however, as it lives in man, is only a shadow picture, a phantom of its true nature. Just as the shadow of an object on the wall is related to the real object that throws this shadow, so is the thought that makes its appearance through a human brain related to the being in the spiritland that corresponds to this thought. Now, when his spiritual sense is awakened, man really perceives this thought being, just as the eye of the senses perceives a table or a chair. He goes about in a region of thought beings. The corporeal eye perceives the lion, and the thinking directed to the sensibly perceptible thinks merely the thought "lion" as a shadow, a shadowy picture. The spiritual eye sees in spiritland the thought "lion" as really and actually as the corporeal eye sees the physical lion. Here we may again refer to the analogy already used regarding the land of the soul. Just as the surroundings of a man born blind and operated upon appear suddenly with the new qualities of color and light, so do the surroundings of the person who learns to use his spiritual eye appear as a new world, the world of living thoughts or spirit beings. In this world there are to be seen, first, the spiritual archetypes of all things and beings that are present in the physical and soul worlds. Imagine a painter's picture existing in his mind before it is painted. This gives an analogy to what is meant by the expression *archetype*. It does not concern us here that the painter has perhaps not had such an archetype in his mind before he paints and that it only gradually develops and becomes complete during the execution of the picture. In the real world of spirit there exist such archetypes for all things, and the physical things and beings are copies of these archetypes. It is quite understandable when anyone who only trusts his outer senses denies this archetypal world and holds that archetypes are merely abstractions gained by an intellectual comparison of sense objects. Such a person simply cannot see in this higher world. He knows the thought world only in its shadowy abstraction. He does not know that the person with spiritual vision is as familiar with spirit beings as he himself is with his dog or his cat, and that the archetypal world has a far more intense reality than the world of the physical senses.

True, the first look into this spiritland is still more bewildering than the first glimpse into the soul world because the archetypes in their true form are very unlike their sensory reflections. They are, however, just as unlike their shadows, the abstract thoughts. In the spiritual world all is in perpetual, mobile activity in the process of ceaseless

103

creating. A state of rest, a remaining in one place such as we find in the physical world, does not exist here because the archetypes are creative beings.* They are the master builders of all that comes into being in the physical and soul worlds. Their forms change rapidly and in each archetype lies the possibility of assuming myriads of specialized forms. They let the different shapes well up out of them, as it were, and no sooner is one produced than the archetype sets about pouring forth the next one from itself. Moreover, the archetypes stand in more or less intimate relationships to each other. They do not work singly. The one requires the help of the other in its creating. Often innumerable archetypes work together in order that this or that being in the soul or physical world may arise.

Besides what is to be perceived by "spiritual sight" in this spiritland, there is something else experienced that is to be regarded as "spiritual hearing." As soon as the clairvoyant rises out of the soul world into the spirit world, the archetypes that are perceptible become "sounding" as well. This sounding, this emission of a tone, is a purely spiritual process. It must be conceived without any accompanying thought of a physical sound. The observer feels as if he were in an ocean of tones, and in these tones, in this spiritual chiming, the beings of the spirit world express themselves. The primordial laws of their existence, their mutual relationships and affinities,

* See *Addendum 9.*

express themselves in the intermingling of these sounds, in their harmonies, melodies and rhythms. What the intellect perceives in the physical world as law, as idea, reveals itself to the spiritual ear as spiritual music. Hence, the Pythagoreans called this perception of the spiritual world the "music of the spheres." To the possessor of a spiritual ear this music of the spheres is not something merely figurative or allegorical, but a spiritual reality well-known to him. If we wish to gain a conception of this spiritual music, however, we must lay aside all ideas of the music of the senses as perceived by the material ear because in spiritual music we are concerned with a spiritual perception, that is, with perception of a kind that must remain silent to the ear of the senses.

In the following descriptions of spiritland reference to this spiritual music will be omitted for the sake of simplicity. We have only to realize that everything described as picture, as shining with light, is at the same time sounding. Each color, each perception of light represents a spiritual tone, and every combination of colors corresponds with a harmony, a melody. Thus we must hold clearly in mind that even where the sounding prevails, perception by means of the spiritual eye by no means ceases. The sounding is merely added to the shining. Therefore, where archetypes are spoken of in the following pages, the primal tones are to be thought of as also present. Other perceptions make their appearance as well, which by way of comparison may be termed spiritual tasting and the like, but it is not proposed to go into these processes here since we are concerned with awakening a conception of spiritland through some few isolated modes of perception selected out of the whole.

Now it is necessary at the outset to distinguish the different species of archetypes from each other. In spiritland also it is necessary to distinguish between a number of degrees or regions in order to find one's way among them. Here also, as in the soul world, the different regions are not to be thought of as laid one above the other like strata, but as mutually interpenetrating and permeating each other.

The First Region. This region contains the archetypes of the physical world insofar as it is devoid of life. The archetypes of the minerals and plants are to be found here, but the archetypes of plants are found only to the extent that they are purely physical, that is, insofar as any life content they may possess is disregarded. In the same way we find here the physical forms of the animals and of men. This by no means exhausts all that is to be found in this region, but merely illustrates it by the most obvious examples. This region forms the basic structure of spiritland. It can be likened to the solid land masses of the physical earth. It forms the continental masses of spiritland. Its relationship with the physical corporeal world can only be described by means of an illustration. Some idea of it can be gained in the following way.

Picture a limited space filled with physical bodies of the most varied kinds. Then think these bodies away and conceive in their stead hollow spaces having their forms. The intervening spaces that were previously empty must be thought of as filled with the most varied forms having manifold relationships with the physical bodies spoken of above. In appearance this is somewhat like the lowest region of the archetypal world. In it the things and beings that become embodied in the physical world are present as hollow spaces, and in the intervening spaces the mobile activity of the archetypes and of the spiritual music takes place. During their formation into physical forms the hollow spaces become, as it were, filled with physical matter. If anyone were to look into space with both physical and spiritual eyes, he would see the physical bodies and between them the mobile activity of the creative archetypes.

The Second Region. This region of spiritland contains the archetypes of life, but this life forms here a perfect unity. It streams through the world of spirit as a fluid element, like blood, pulsating through everything. It may be likened to the sea and the water systems of the physical earth. Its distribution, however, is more like the distribution of the blood in the animal body than that of the seas and rivers. One could describe this second stage of the spiritland as flowing life composed of thought substance. In this element are the creative primal forces producing

107

everything that appears in physical reality as living beings. Here it becomes evident that all life is a unity, that the life in man is related to the life of all his fellow creatures.

The Third Region. The archetypes of all soul formations must be designated as the third region of the spiritland. Here we find ourselves in a much finer and rarer element than in the first two regions. To use a comparison it can be called the air or atmosphere of spiritland. Everything that goes on in the souls of both the other worlds—the physical and soul worlds—has here its spiritual counterpart. Here all feelings, sensations, instincts and passions are again present, but spiritually present. The atmospheric events in this aerial region correspond to the sorrows and joys of the creatures in the other worlds. The longing of the human soul appears here as a gentle zephyr; an outbreak of passion is like a stormy blast. He who can visualize what is here under consideration pierces deep into the sighing of every creature if he directs his attention to the matter. We can, for example, speak here of a loud storm with flashing lightning and rolling thunder. If we investigate the matter further, we find that the passions of a battle waged on earth are expressed in spiritland in a storm of spirit beings.

The Fourth Region. The archetypes of the fourth region are not immediately related to the other worlds. They are in certain respects beings who govern the archetypes of the three lower regions and mediate their working together. They are accordingly occupied with the ordering and grouping of these subordinate archetypes. Therefore, a more comprehensive activity proceeds from this region than from the lower ones.

The Fifth, Sixth and Seventh Regions. These regions differ essentially from the preceding ones because the beings to be found in them supply the archetypes of the lower regions with the impulses to their activity. In them we find the creative forces of the archetypes themselves. Whoever is able to rise to these regions makes acquaintance with purposes that underlie our world.* Like living germ-points, the archetypes still lie here ready to assume the most manifold forms of thought beings. If these germ-points are projected into the lower regions, they well up, as it were, and manifest themselves in the most varied shapes. The ideas through which the human spirit manifests itself creatively in the physical world are the reflection, the shadow, of these germinal thought beings of the higher spiritual world. The observer with the spiritual ear who rises from the lower regions of spiritland to these higher ranges becomes aware that sounds and tones are transformed into a spiritual language. He begins to perceive the Spiritual Word through which the things and beings no longer make known to him their nature in music

* That such a term as "purposes" can also only be used in the sense of a "simile" is obviously self-explanatory from what was said above about the difficulties of expressing in language such thoughts as these. The last thing intended is to warm over the old "doctrine of purpose." See also *Addendum 10.*

109

alone, but now express it in words. They utter what can be called in spiritual science their *eternal names.**

We must visualize these thought germ-beings as possessing a composite nature. Only the germ-sheath is taken out of the element of the thought world, and this surrounds the true life kernel. With it we have reached the confines of the three worlds because the kernel has its origin in still higher worlds. When man was described in the preceding pages according to his component parts, this life kernel of his was mentioned and its components were called *life spirit* and *spirit man*. There are similar life kernels for other beings in the cosmos. They originate in higher worlds and are placed in the three that have been described in order to accomplish their tasks in them.

The human spirit will now be followed on its further pilgrimage through spiritland between two embodiments or incarnations. While doing this the conditions and distinguishing characteristics of this "land" will once more come clearly into view.

4. *The Spirit in Spiritland after Death*

When the human spirit has passed through the world of souls on its way between two incarnations, it enters the land of spirits to remain there until it is ripe for a new bodily existence. One can only understand the meaning of this sojourn in spiritland when one is able to interpret in

* See *Addendum 11*.

110

the right way the aim and end of the pilgrimage of man through his incarnation. While man is incarnated in the physical body he works and creates in the physical world as a spiritual being. He imprints on the physical forms, on corporeal materials and forces what his spirit thinks out and develops. As a messenger of the spiritual world he has, therefore, to embody the spirit in the corporeal world. Only by being embodied, incarnated, can man work in the world of bodies. He must take on the physical body as his tool so that through the body he can act on other bodies and they on him. What acts through this physical corporeality of man is the spirit. From this spirit flow the purposes, the direction its work is to take in the physical world.

Now as long as the spirit works in the physical body, it cannot as spirit live in its true form. It can, as it were, only shine through the veil of physical existence because, as a matter of fact, the thought life of man really belongs to the spiritual world. As it appears in physical existence its true form is veiled. It can also be said that the thought life of the physical man is a shadow, a reflection of the true, spiritual being to whom it belongs. Thus, during physical life, the spirit working through the physical body interacts with the earthly corporeal world. Although one of the tasks of the human spirit, as long as it proceeds from incarnation to incarnation, is to work upon the physical corporeal world, it could by no means fulfill this task in a proper manner if it lived merely in embodied exist-

111

ence. The purposes and goals of the earthly task are just as little developed and determined within the earthly incarnation, as the plan of a house comes into existence on the site where the laborers work. Just as this plan is worked out in the office of the architect, so are the aims and purposes of earthly creative activities worked out and developed in the land of spirits. The spirit of man has to live again and again in this land between two incarnations in order to be able, equipped with what he takes with him on his departure, to approach the work in the physical life. Just as the architect, without working with brick and mortar, works out the plan of the house in his drafting room in accordance with architectural and other laws, so too does the architect of human creation, the spirit or higher self, develop its capacities and aims in spiritland in accordance with the laws of that land, in order to bring them over into the earthly world. Only when the human spirit sojourns again and again in its own region, will it also be able by means of the physical corporeal instruments to bring the spirit into the earthly world.

On the physical scene of action man learns to know the qualities and forces of the physical world. During his creative activity he gathers experiences regarding the demands made by the physical world on anyone wishing to work in it. He learns to know there, as it were, the qualities of the matter in which he wishes to embody his thoughts and ideas. The thoughts and ideas themselves he

112

cannot extract from matter. Thus the physical world is both the scene of his creating and of his learning. In the spiritland, what has been learned is then transformed into living faculties of the spirit. One can carry the above comparison farther in order to make the matter clearer. The architect designs a house. His plans are carried out. In doing this he gains the most varied experiences. All of these experiences enhance his capacities. When he works out his next design, all these experiences flow into it, and this next design, when compared to the first, is seen to be enriched with all that was learned through the first.

It is the same with the successive human lives. In the intervals between incarnations, the spirit lives in its own sphere. It can give itself up entirely to the requirements of the spirit life. Freed from the physical body, it develops itself in every direction and works into this development the fruits of its experiences in former earthly careers. Thus its attention is always directed to the scene of its earthly tasks. Thus it works continually at following the earth insofar as that is its field of action, through its necessary development. It works upon itself in order to be able in each incarnation to carry out its service during that life in accordance with the condition of the earth at that time. This is, of course, only a general outline of successive human lives. Reality will never quite correspond with it, but only to a certain degree. Circumstances may decree that a man's subsequent life be much less perfect than a previous one, but taken as a whole such irregularities equalize themselves in the succession of lives within definite limits.

The development of the spirit in spiritland takes place in consequence of man's entering completely into the life of the various regions of this land. His own life dissolves, as it were, into these regions successively and he takes on, for the time being, their characteristics. Through this they penetrate his being with theirs in order that he may be able to work, strengthened by theirs, in his earthly life.

In the *first region* of spiritland man is surrounded by the spiritual archetypes of earthly things. During life on earth he learns to know only the shadows of these archetypes that he grasps in his thoughts. What is merely thought on the earth is in this region experienced, lived. Man moves among thoughts, but these thoughts are real beings. What he has perceived with his senses during life on earth acts on him now in its thought form. The thought, however, does not appear as the shadow hiding itself behind the things. It is, on the contrary, the life-filled reality producing the things. Man is, as it were, in the thought workshop in which earthly things are formed and fashioned, because in the land of spirit all is vital activity and mobility. Here the thought world is at work as a world of living beings, creative and constructive. We see how what we have experienced during the earthly existence is constructed. Just as in the physical body we experience the things of the senses as reality, so now, as

114

spirit, we experience the spiritual, constructive forces as real.

Among the thought beings to be found in spiritland is also the thought of our own physical corporeality. We feel removed from the latter. We feel only the spiritual being as belonging to ourselves, and when we perceive the discarded body as if in memory, no longer as physical but as thought being, then its relation to the external world becomes a matter of direct perception. We learn to look at it as something belonging to the external world, as a member of this external world. We consequently no longer distinguish our own corporeality from the rest of the external world as something more closely related to ourselves. We feel the unity in the whole external world including our own bodily incarnations. Our own embodiments dissolve here into a unity with the rest of the world. Thus man here looks upon the archetypes of the physical corporeal reality as a unity to which he has belonged himself. He learns, therefore, gradually to know his relationship, his unity with the surrounding world by observation. He learns to say to it, "What is here spread out around thee, thou wert that." This is one of the fundamental thoughts of ancient Indian Vedanta wisdom. The sage acquires, even during his earthly life, what others experience after death, namely, the ability to grasp the thought that he himself is related to all things—the thought, "Thou art that." In earthly life this is an ideal to which the thought life can be devoted. In the land of the spirit it is an immediate fact, one that grows ever clearer to us through spiritual experience, and man himself comes to know ever more clearly in this land that in his own inner being he belongs to the spirit world. He perceives himself to be a spirit among spirits, a member of the primordial spirits, feeling within himself the word of the primordial spirit, "I am the Primal Spirit." The wisdom of the Vedanta says, "I am Brahman," that is, I belong as a member to the primordial being in whom all beings have their origin. We see that what is grasped during earthly life as a shadowy thought towards which all wisdom strives is in spiritland an immediate experience. Indeed, it is only *thought* during earth life because it is a *fact* in spiritual existence.

Thus man during his spiritual existence sees as if from outside from a high watch tower the relationships and facts in the midst of which he stands during his earthly life. During his life in the lowest region of spiritland, he lives in regard to the eartly relationships immediately connected with physical corporeal reality. On earth man is born into a family, a folk; he lives in a certain country. His earthly existence is determed by all these relationships. He finds this or that friend because relationships within the physical world bring it about. He carries on this or that business. All this decides the conditions of his earthly life. All this presents itself to him during his life in the first region of spiritland as living thought being. He lives it all through again in a certain way, but he lives it through from the active spiritual side. The fam-

116

ily love he has exercised, the friendship he has produced, become alive and quick from within, and his capacities in this direction are enhanced. That element in the spirit of man that acts as the force of love of family and friend is strengthened. He later enters on his earthly existence again as a more perfect man in these respects. It is to a certain extent the everyday relationships of earth life that ripen as the fruit of this lowest region of spiritland. That element in man, which in its interests is wholly absorbed by these everyday relationships, will feel itself in affinity with this region for the greater part of its life between two incarnations. We find again in the spiritual world the people with whom we have lived in the physical world. Just as everything loosens and falls away from the soul that was peculiarly its own through the physical body, so also does the bond that in physical life linked soul with soul loosen itself from those conditions that have meaning and effectiveness only in the physical world. Yet all that soul was to soul in physical life is carried over beyond death into the spiritual world. It is natural that words coined for physical conditions can only reproduce inaccurately what takes place in the spiritual world. If this is taken into account, it must be described as quite correct when it is said that those souls that belong together in physical life find each other again in order to continue in a corresponding manner their joint lives in the spiritual world.

In the *second region* the common life of the earth world flows as thought being, as a fluid element, so to speak, of spiritland. As long as one observes the world during physical embodiment, life appears to be confined within separate living beings. In spiritland it is liberated from them and, like life-blood, flows as it were through the whole land. It exists there as the living unity that is present in all things. Of this also only a reflection appears to man during earthly life, and this reflection expresses itself in every form of reverence that he pays to the whole, to the unity and harmony of the universe. The religious life of man is derived from this reflection. He becomes aware of how far the all-embracing meaning of existence does not lie in what is transitory and separate. He regards the transitory as a similitude, a likeness of an eternal, harmonious unity. He looks up to this unity in a mood of reverence and worship. He performs before it religious rites and ceremonies. In spiritland, not the reflection but the real form appears as living thought being. Here man can really join himself to the unity that he has reverenced on earth. The fruits of religious life and all connected with it make their appearance in this region. Man now learns through spiritual experience to recognize that his individual destiny is not to be separated from the community to which he belongs. The capacity to know oneself as a member of a whole develops here. The religious feelings, all that has already during life striven after a pure and noble morality, will draw strength out of this region during a great part of the spiritual life between incarnations, and a man will reincarnate with enhanced capacities in this direction.

118

While in the first region we are in company of those souls with whom we have been linked by the closest ties of the physical world during the preceding physical life, in the second region we enter the domain of all those with whom we felt united in a wider sense, that is, through a common reverence, through a common religious confession, and so on. It must be emphasized that the spiritual experiences of the preceding regions continue to persist through the subsequent ones. Thus man is not at all torn away from the ties knitted by family, friendship, and so on, when he enters upon the life of the second and following regions. Moreover, the regions of spiritland do not lie like sections one beside the other. They interpenetrate each other, and man experiences himself in a new region not because he has externally entered upon it in any form whatever, but because he has attained in himself the inner capacities for now perceiving what he previously lived within, but without perceiving it.

The *third region* of spiritland contains the archetypes of the soul world. All that lives in this world is here present as living thought being. We find in it the archetypes of desires, wishes and feelings, but here in the spirit world nothing self-seeking clings to the soul. Just as all life forms a unity in the second region, so in this third region all longings, wishes, all likes and dislikes form a unity. The desire and wish of others are not separable from my desire and wish. The sensations and feelings of all beings are a common world, enclosing and surrounding every-

119

thing else, just as the physical atmosphere surrounds the earth. This region is, as it were, the atmosphere or air of spiritland. All that a person has carried out in his life on earth in the service of the community, in selfless devotion to his fellowmen, will bear fruit here because through this service, through this self-giving, he has lived in a reflection of the third region of spiritland. The great benefactors of the human race, the self-sacrificing natures, those who render great services to communities, have gained their ability to render them in this region after having acquired for themselves the readiness for a special relation to it during their previous earthly careers.

It is evident that the three regions of spiritland just described stand in a certain relation to the worlds below them, to the physical and soul worlds, because they contain the archetypes, the living thought beings, that take up corporeal or soul existence in those worlds. Only the *fourth region* is the pure spiritland, but even this region is not quite that in the fullest sense of the word. It differs from the three lower regions owing to the fact that in them we meet with the archetypes of those physical and soul relations that man finds existing in the physical and soul worlds before he himself begins to participate in them. The circumstances of everyday life link themselves with the things and beings that man finds already present in the world. The transitory things of this world direct his gaze to their eternal primal foundation, and his fellow creatures also, to whom he selflessly devotes himself, do not owe their presence to him. It is, however, through him that there are in the world all the creations of the arts, sciences, engineering, states and governments—in short, all that he has embodied in the world as original creations of his spirit. Without his activity these could not manifest themselves in the physical world. The archetypes of these purely human creations are in the fourth region of the spiritland. All that we develop during earthly life in the way of scientific discoveries, of artistic ideas and forms, of technical conceptions, bears fruit in this fourth region. It is out of this region therefore that artists, scientists and inventors draw their impulses and enhance their genius during their stay in spiritland in order during another incarnation to be able to assist in fuller measure the further evolution of human culture. But we must not imagine that this fourth region of spiritland possesses importance only for specially prominent human beings. It has great importance for all men. All that occupies us in our physical life outside the sphere of everyday living, wishing and willing has its source in this region. If we did not pass through it in the period between death and a new birth, we would in our subsequent life have no interests leading out beyond the narrow circle of our personal life-conduct to what is common to all humanity.

It has already been said above that even this region cannot be called pure spiritland in the full sense of the word. This is the case because the stage at which men have left civilization on earth continues to influence their spiritual existence. They can enjoy in spiritland only the fruits of what it was possible for them to carry out in accordance with their talents and the stage of development of the folk, state and nation into which they were born.

In the still higher regions of the spiritland the human spirit is now freed from every earthly fetter. It rises to the pure spiritland in which it experiences the intentions, the aims, that the spirit set itself to accomplish by means of the earthly life. All that has been already realized in the earthly world brings into existence only a more or less weak copy of the highest intentions and aims. Each crystal, each tree, each animal, and all that is being realized in the domain of human creation—all this gives only copies of what the spirit intends, and man during his incarnations can only link himself with these imperfect copies of the perfect intentions and aims. Thus during one of his incarnations he himself can only be an image of what, in the kingdom of the spirit, he is intended to be. What he really is as spirit in spiritland comes, therefore, into view only when he rises to the *fifth region* of spiritland in the interval between two incarnations. What he is here is really he himself—the being who receives an external existence in the numerous and varied incarnations. In this region the true self of man can freely live and expand in all directions, and this self is thus the being who appears ever anew in each incarnation as the one. This self brings with it the faculties that have developed in the lower regions of the spiritland. It consequently carries the fruits of former lives over into those following. It is the bearer of the results of former incarnations.

When the self lives in the fifth region of the spiritland, it is in the kingdom of intentions and purposes. Just as the architect learns from the imperfections that have come to light in his work, and just as he brings into his new designs only what he was able to change from imperfections to perfections, so does the self in the fifth region discard from the results of its former lives whatever is bound up with the imperfections of the lower worlds, and with these results it impregnates the purposes of the spiritland—purposes with which it now lives. It is clear that the force that can be drawn from this region will depend upon how much the self during its incarnation has acquired in the form of results fit to be taken up into the world of purposes. The self that has sought to realize the purposes of the spirit during earthly life through an active thought life, or through wise love expressed in deeds, will establish a strong claim upon this region. The self that has expended its efforts entirely on the events of everyday life, that has lived only in the transitory, has sown no seeds that can be fruitful in the purposes of the eternal world order. Only the small portion of its activities that extended beyond the interests of everyday life can unfold as fruit in these higher regions of the spiritland. It must not be supposed that what comes into consideration here is chiefly earthly fame or anything akin to it. No, the important thing to realize here is that in the narrowest walks of life even the least

123

event has its significance in the eternal progressive course of existence.

We must make ourselves familiar with the thought that in this region our judgments must be different from those in the physical life. For instance, if a man has acquired little that is related to this fifth region, the craving arises in him to imprint an impulse upon himself for the following life that will cause that life to run its course in such a way that in its destiny (karma) the corresponding effect of that deficiency will come to light. Experiences, which in the following earth life appear as a painful destiny, seen from that life—and perhaps deeply bewailed as such—are, nevertheless, the very experiences that a man in this region of spiritland finds absolutely necessary for himself.

Since a man in the fifth region lives in his own true self, he is lifted out of everything from the lower worlds that envelops him during his incarnations. He is what he ever was and ever will be during the course of his incarnations. He lives in the governing power of the intentions that prevail during these incarnations, and that he grafts into his own self. He looks back on his own past and feels that all he has experienced in it will be brought into service in the intentions he has to realize in the future. There flash forth a kind of remembrance of his earlier, and a prophetic vision of his future lives. We see, therefore, that what we call in this book *spirit self* lives in this region, as far as it is developed, in the reality that is appropriate to it. It develops itself still further and prepares itself to make possible in a new incarnation the fulfillment of the spiritual intentions in the realities of earthly life.

If, during a succession of sojourns in spiritland, the spirit self has evolved so far that it can move about quite freely there, it will evermore seek there its true home. Life in the world of spirit will be as familiar to it as life in physical reality is to the earthly man. The view-points of the spirit world operate from now on as the dominating ones, which it makes its own more or less consciously or unconsciously for its succeeding earth lives. The self can feel itself to be a member of the divine world order. The limitations and laws of the earthly life do not affect it in its innermost being. Power for all that it carries out comes to it from this spiritual world. The spiritual world, however, is a unity. He who lives in it knows how the Eternal has worked creatively upon the past. Out of the Eternal he can determine the direction for the future.* His view over the past widens into a perfect one. The man who has reached this stage sets before himself aims that he intends to carry out in a coming incarnation. From out the spiritland he influences his future so that it runs its course in harmony with the true and spiritual. Such a person during the stages between two incarnations finds himself in the presence of all those exalted beings before whose gaze divine wisdom lies spread out unveiled, because he has climbed up to the stage at which he can understand it.

In the *sixth region* of the spiritland a man will fulfill in

---

* See *Addendum 12.*

125

all his actions what is most in accord with the true being
of the world. He cannot seek after what profits himself,
but only after what ought to happen according to the right
course of the world order.

In the *seventh region* of the spiritland the limit of the
three worlds is reached. Man stands in the presence of the
life-kernels, which are transplanted from higher worlds
into the three already described in order that in them they
may fulfill their tasks. When a man has reached the
boundary of the three worlds, he recognizes himself in his
own life-kernel. This implies that for him the problems of
these three worlds have been solved. He has a complete
view of the entire life of these worlds. In physical life the
powers of the soul, through which it obtains the experiences in the spiritual world here described, remain unconscious under ordinary circumstances. They work in
their unconscious depths upon the bodily organs, which
bring about the consciousness of the physical world. That
is precisely the reason why these powers remain imperceptible for this world. The eye, too, does not see itself because forces are at work in it that make other things
visible. If one would judge to what extent a human life
running its course between birth and death can be the result of preceding earth lives, one must take into consideration the fact that a point of view that lies within this same
life, and at the outset is the natural one, can yield no possibility of correct judgment. For such a point of view, for
instance, an earth life could appear full of suffering,

imperfect. Yet, seen from an extra-earthly view-point, this very configuration of the earth life with its suffering, its imperfections, would prove to be the result of previous earth lives. By treading the path of knowledge as this is described in the next chapter, the soul sets itself free from the conditions of bodily life. Thus it can perceive in a picture the experiences that it undergoes between death and a new birth. Perception of this kind makes it possible to describe what happens in spiritland as has been done here in but little more than outline. Only when we do not neglect to hold before our minds the fact that the whole disposition of the soul is different in the physical body from its disposition during purely spiritual experiences, only then shall we see the description given here in the right light.

5. The Physical World and Its Connection With the Soul and Spiritland

The formations in the soul world and in spiritland cannot be the objects of external sense perception. The objects of this sense perception are to be added as a third world to the two already described. Man lives during his bodily existence simultaneously in the three worlds. He perceives the things of the sensory world and acts upon them. The formations of the soul world act upon him through their forces of sympathy and antipathy, and his own soul excites waves in the soul world by its likes and dislikes, desires and wishes. The spiritual being of things, on the other hand, mirrors itself in his thought world and he himself, as thinking spirit-being, is a citizen of spiritland and a companion of all that lives in that region of the world. This makes it evident that the sensory world is only a part of what surrounds us. This part stands out from our general surrounding with a certain independence because it can be perceived by senses that disregard the soul and spiritual parts. These, however, belong just as much to this surrounding world as does the material part. Just as a piece of floating ice is substance of the surrounding water although it stands out prominently owing to particular qualities, so are the things perceptible to the senses substance of the surrounding soul and spirit worlds. They stand out from these worlds owing to particular qualities that make them perceptible to the senses. They are, speaking somewhat metaphorically, condensed spirit and soul formations, and the condensation makes it possible for the senses to acquire knowledge of them. In fact, just as ice is only a form in which water exists, so are the objects of the senses only a form in which soul and spirit beings exist. If this has been grasped, it can also be understood that as water can pass over into ice, so the spirit world can pass over into the soul world, and the soul world into that of the senses.

Looked at from this point of view it can be seen why we can form thoughts about the things of the senses. Thus, there is a question that everyone who thinks must ask himself, "In what relation does the thought that we have about a stone stand to the stone itself?" This question rises in full clearness in the minds of those persons who look with especial penetration into external nature. They feel the consonance of the human thought world with the structure and order of nature. The great astronomer, Kepler, for example, speaks in a beautiful way about this harmony. He says, "True it is that the divine call that bids man study astronomy stands written in the world, not indeed in words and syllables, but factually by virtue of the adaptability of the human senses and concepts to the concatenations of the heavenly bodies and conditions." Only because the things of the sensible world are nothing but condensed spirit beings is the man who lifts himself by means of his thoughts to these spirit beings able by thinking to understand the things. Sense objects originate in the spirit world. They are only another form of the spirit beings, and when a man forms thoughts about things, his inner nature is merely directed away from the sensible form and out towards the spiritual archetypes of these things. To understand an object by means of thought is a process that may be likened to the lique-faction of a solid body by fire in order that the chemist may examine it in its liquid form.

The spiritual archetypes of the sense world are to be found in the various regions of the spiritland. In the fifth, sixth and seventh regions these archetypes are still found as living germ-points. In the four lower regions they

129

shape themselves into spiritual structures. The human spirit perceives a shadowy reflection of these spiritual formations when by thinking it tries to gain understanding of the things of the senses. How these formations have condensed until they form the sense world is a problem for the seeker who strives towards a spiritual understanding of the world around him.

For human sense perception this surrounding world is divided primarily into four distinctly separate stages—the mineral, plant, animal and human. The *mineral kingdom* is perceived by the senses and comprehended by thought. Thus, when we form a thought about a mineral body, we have to do with two things—the sense object and the thought. Accordingly, we must imagine that this sense object is a condensed thought being. Now, one mineral being acts on another in an external way. It impinges on it and moves it. It warms it, lights it up, dissolves it, and so forth. This external kind of action can be expressed in thoughts. We form thoughts about the way mineral things act on each other externally in accordance with law. By this means our separate thoughts expand into a thought picture of the whole mineral world, and this thought picture is a reflection of the archetype of the whole mineral world of the senses. It is to be found as a complete whole in the spirit world.

In the *plant kingdom* the phenomena of growth and propagation are added to the phenomenon of external action of one thing or another. The plant grows and

130

brings forth from itself beings like itself. Life is here added to what confronts us in the mineral kingdom. The simple recollection of this fact leads to a view that is enlightening in this connection. The plant has the power to create its living shape and to reproduce it in a being of its own kind. In between the shapeless character of mineral matter as we meet it in gases, liquids, etc., and the living shape of the plant world, stand the forms of the crystals. In the crystals we have to seek the transition from the shapeless mineral world to the plant kingdom that has the capacity for forming living shapes. In this externally sensory formative process in both kingdoms, mineral and plant, we must see the sensory condensation of the purely spiritual process that takes place when the spiritual germs of the three higher regions of the spiritland form themselves into the spirit shapes of the lower regions. The transition from the formless spiritual germ to the formed structure corresponds in the spiritual world to the process of crystallization. This transition is the spiritual archetype of the process of crystallization. If this transition condenses so that the senses can perceive it in its outcome, it then exhibits itself in the world of senses as the process of mineral crystallization.

There is, however, also in the plant being a fashioned spirit germ. Here the living, fashioning capacity is still retained in the shaped being. In the crystal the spirit germ has lost its constructive power during the process of fashioning. It has exhausted its life in the shape produced.

131

The plant has shape and in addition it has the capacity to produce a shape. The characteristic belonging to the spirit germs in the higher regions of the spiritland has been preserved in the plant life. The plant has, therefore, form like the crystal, and to that is added the shaping or formative force. Besides the form that the primal beings have assumed in the plant shape, there is another form working on that shape that bears the impress of the spirit beings of the higher regions. Only what manifests itself in the completed shape of the plant, however, is sensibly perceptible. The formative beings who give life to this shape are present but imperceptible in the plant kingdom. The physical eye sees the lily small today and some time later sees it grown larger. The formative force that evolves the latter out of the former is not seen by this eye. This formative force being is the part of the plant world that acts imperceptibly to the senses. The spirit germs have descended a stage in order to work in the kingdom of shapes. In spiritual science elementary kingdoms are spoken of. If we designate the primal forms, which have as yet no shape, as the *first elementary kingdom,* then the force beings who work invisible to the senses as the craftsmen of plant growth may be designated as belonging to the *second elementary kingdom.*

In the *animal world* sensation and impulse are added to the capacities for growth and propagation. These are manifestations of the soul world. A being endowed with

132

these belongs to the soul world, receives impressions from it and reacts on it. Now, every sensation and every impulse that arises in the animal is brought forth from the foundations of the animal soul. The shape is more enduring than the feeling or impulse. One may say that the life of sensation bears the same relation to the more enduring living shape that the self-changing plant shape bears to the rigid crystal. The plant exhausts itself to a certain extent in the shape-forming force; during its life it continues to add new shapes to itself. First it sends forth roots, then its leafy structure, later flowers, and finally its fruit and seeds. The animal is enclosed within a shape complete within itself and develops within this the changeful life of feeling and impulse. This life has its existence in the soul world. The plant grows and propagates itself; the animal feels and develops its impulses. They constitute for the animal the formless that is always developing into new forms. They have their archetypal processes ultimately in the highest regions of spiritland, but they carry out their activities in the soul world. There are thus in the animal world in addition to the force beings who, invisible to the senses, direct growth and propagation, others who have descended a stage deeper into the soul world. In the animal kingdom formless beings who clothe themselves in soul sheaths are present as the master builders bringing about sensations and impulses. They are the real architects of the animal

133

forms. In spiritual science this region to which they belong may be called the *third elementary kingdom.*

Man, in addition to having the capacities named in plant and animal, is furnished also with the power of elaborating his sensations into ideas and thoughts and of controlling his impulses by thinking. The thought, which appears in the plant as shape and in the animal as soul force, makes its appearance in man in its own form as thought itself. The animal is soul; man is spirit. The spirit being, which in the animal is engaged in soul development, has now descended a stage deeper still. In the animal it is soul forming. In man it has entered into the world of sensory matter itself. The spirit is present within the human sensory body, and because it appears in a sensory garment, it can appear only as the shadowy reflection of the spirit being that thought represents. The spirit manifests in man conditioned by the physical brain organism, but at the same time it has become the inner being of man. Thought is the form that the formless spirit being assumes in man, just as it takes on shape in the plant and soul in the animal. Consequently, man, insofar as he is a thinking being, is subject to no elementary kingdom fashioning him from without. His elementary kingdom works in his physical body. Only to the extent that man is shape and sentient being is he worked upon by elementary beings of the same kind as those working upon plants and animals. The thought organism of man is elaborated entirely from

134

within his physical body. In the spirit organism of man, in his nervous system that has developed into the perfect brain, we have sensibly visible before us what works on plants and animals as non-sensory force being. That is, the animal shows self-feeling, but man self-consciousness. In the animal, spirit feels itself as soul. It does not yet grasp itself as spirit. In man, the spirit recognizes itself as spirit although, owing to physical limitations, merely as a shadowy reflection of the spirit, as thought.

The threefold world, accordingly, falls into the following categories:

1. Realm of archetypal formless beings—first elementary kingdom.
2. Realm of shape-creating beings—second elementary kingdom.
3. Realm of soul beings—third elementary kingdom.
4. Realm of created shapes (crystal forms)—mineral kingdom.
5. Realm whose forms are sensibly perceptible and in which the shape-creating beings are active—plant kingdom.
6. Realm whose forms are sensibly perceptible and in which the shape-creating and soul beings are active —animal kingdom.
7. Realm whose forms are sensibly perceptible and in which the shape-creating and soul beings are active,

135

and in which the spirit fashions itself in the form of thought within the sense world—human kingdom.

From this can be seen how the basic constituents of man living in the body are connected with the spiritual world. The physical body, the ether body, the sentient soul body and the intellectual soul are to be regarded as archetypes of the spiritland condensed in the sensory world. The physical body comes into existence through condensation of the human archetype to the point of sensory appearance. For this reason one can call this physical body also a being of the first elementary kingdom condensed to sensory perceptibility. The ether body comes into existence through the fact that the shape thus engendered maintains its mobility through a being that extends its activity into the kingdom of the senses but is not itself visible to the senses. If one wishes to character- ize this being fully, it must be described as having its origin in the highest regions of spiritland and thence shap- ing itself in the second region into an archetype of life. As such an archetype of life it works in the sensory world. In a similar way, the being that builds up the sentient soul body has its origin in the highest regions of the spiritland, forms itself in the third spirit region into the archetype of the soul world, and as such works in the sensory world. The intellectual soul, however, comes into existence when in the fourth region of the spiritland the archetype of the thinking man gives itself a thought form in which it acts directly as thinking man in the world of the senses. Thus man stands within the world of the senses. Thus the spirit works on his physical body, ether body and sentient soul body. Thus this spirit comes into manifestation in the intellectual soul. Archetypes in the form of beings who in a certain sense are external to man work upon the three lower members of his being. In his intellectual soul he himself becomes a conscious worker upon himself. The beings who work on his physical body are the same as those who form mineral nature. Beings of the kind that live in the plant kingdom work on his ether body, and those beings such as live in the animal kingdom work on his sentient soul body. Both are imperceptible to the senses but extend their activity into these kingdoms.

Thus do the different worlds combine in action. The universe man lives in is the expression of this combined activity.

* * *

When we have grasped the sensory world in this way, the understanding opens up for beings of a kind different from those having their existence in the above mentioned four kingdoms of nature. One example of such beings is what may be called the Folk or National Spirit. This being does not manifest itself directly in a sensibly perceptible way, but lives its life entirely in the sensations, feelings, tendencies and impulses observable in the common

137

characteristics of a whole nation. This is a being who does not incarnate in the sense world, but just as man forms his body out of substances sensibly visible, so does this Folk Spirit form its body out of the substance of the soul world. This soul body of the National Spirit is like a cloud in which the members of a nation live. Its influences become evident in the souls of the men concerned, but it does not originate in these souls themselves. The National Spirit remains merely a shadowy conception of the mind without being or life, an empty abstraction, to the man who does not picture it in this way.

Something similar may be said in reference to what one calls the Spirit of the Age (*Zeitgeist*). Indeed, the spiritual outlook is extended in this way over a variety of other beings, both lower and higher, that live in the human environment unseen by the bodily senses. Those who have powers of spiritual sight perceive such beings and can describe them. To the lower species of such beings belongs all that is described by observers of the spiritual world as *salamanders, sylphs, undines* and *gnomes*. It should not be necessary to say that such descriptions are not to be considered reproductions of the reality that underlies them. If they were, then the world in question would be not a spiritual, but a grossly sensory one. They are attempts at making clear a spiritual reality that can only be represented in this way, that is, by similes. It is quite comprehensible that anyone who admits the validity of physical vision only, regards such beings as the offspring of

138

confused fantasy and superstition. They can, of course, never become visible to the sensory eye because they have no sensory bodies. The superstition does not consist in regarding such beings as real, but in believing that they appear in a way perceptible to the physical senses. Beings of such forms co-operate in the construction of the world, and we come into contact with them as soon as we enter the higher regions closed to the bodily senses. Those people are not superstitious who see in such descriptions pictures of spiritual realities, but rather those who believe in the sensory existence of the pictures, as well as those who deny the spirit, because they think they must deny the sensory picture.

Mention must also be made of those beings who do not descend to the soul world, but whose vestment is composed of the formations of spiritland alone. Man perceives them and becomes their companion when he opens his spiritual eye and ear to them. Through such an opening much becomes intelligible to him that previously he could only stare at uncomprehendingly. It becomes bright around him, and he sees the primal causes of what takes place as effects in the world of the senses. He comprehends what he either denied entirely when he had no spiritual eye, or in reference to which he had to content himself with saying, "There are more things in heaven and earth than are dreamed of in thy philosophy." People with fine, spiritual feelings become uneasy when they begin to have a glimmering, when they become vaguely aware of a world different from the sensory one surrounding them, one in which they have to grope about as the blind grope among visible objects. Nothing but the clear vision of these higher regions of existence and a thorough understanding and penetration of what takes place in them can really fortify a man and lead him to his proper goal. Through insight into what lies hidden from the senses, man expands his nature in such a way that he feels his life prior to this expansion as "a mere dreaming about the world."

6. Thought Forms and the Human Aura*

It has been said that the formations of any one of the three worlds can have reality for man only when he has the capacities or the organs for perceiving them. He perceives certain occurrences in space as light phenomena only because he has a correctly constructed eye. How much of what really exists reveals itself to a being depends upon his receptivity. A man, therefore, should never say that what is real is only what he can perceive. Much can be real that he cannot perceive for lack of organs.

Now, the soul world and the spirit world are just as real as the sensory world. Indeed, they are real in a much higher sense. No physical eye can see feelings and thoughts, yet they are real. Just as man by means of his outer senses has the corporeal world before him as an

* See *Addendum 13*.

object of perception, so do feelings, instincts and thoughts become objects of perception for his spiritual organs. Exactly as occurrences in space can be seen with the sensory eye as color phenomena, so can the above named soul and spiritual occurrences become, by means of the inner senses, perceptions that are analogous to the sensory color phenomena. To understand fully in what sense this is meant is only possible for one who has followed the path of knowledge described in the following chapter and has as a result developed his inner senses. For such a person the psychic phenomena in the soul region surrounding him, and the spiritual phenomena in the spiritual region, become supersensibly visible. The feelings of other beings that he experiences ray out to him from them like light phenomena, and thoughts to which he directs his attention surge through spiritual space. For him, the thought of one man about another is not something imperceptible but, on the contrary, is a perceptible occurrence. The content of a thought lives as such only in the soul of the thinker, but this content excites effects in the spirit world. They are the perceptible occurrence to the spiritual eye. The thought streams out as an actual reality from one man and flows to the other, and the way this thought acts on the other person is experienced as a perceptible occurrence in the spiritual world. Thus the physically perceptible man is only part of the whole man for the one whose spiritual senses are unfolded. This physical man becomes the center of soul and spiritual outpourings. It is impossible to do more than faintly indicate the richly varied world that discloses itself here to the seer. A human thought, which otherwise lives only in the understanding of the listener, appears, for example, as a spiritually perceptible color phenomenon. Its color corresponds with the character of the thought. A thought that springs forth from a sensual impulse in a person has a different color from a thought conceived in the service of pure knowledge, noble beauty or the eternally good. Thoughts that spring from the sensual life course through the soul world in shades of red. A thought by which the thinker rises to higher knowledge appears in beautiful light yellow. A thought that springs from devoted and unselfish love rays out in glorious rose red. Just as the content of a thought comes to expression in its supersensibly visible form, so also does the greater or lesser degree of its definiteness. The precise thought of the thinker shows itself as a formation with definite outlines; the confused idea appears as a wavering, cloudy formation.

In this way the soul and spirit nature of man appear as the supersensible part of the whole human being.

The color effects perceptible to the spirit eye that ray out around the physical man observed in his activity, and that envelop him like a somewhat egg-shaped cloud, are the human aura. The size of this aura varies in different people, but we may say that the entire man appears on the average twice as long and four times as wide as the physical man.

142

The most varied shades of color flood the aura. This color flooding is a true picture of the inner human life. As this changes, so do the shades of color change. Certain permanent qualities such as talents, habits and traits of character, however, express themselves also in permanent fundamental color shades.

Misunderstandings can arise in men who at present stand remote from the experiences of the path of knowledge described in a later chapter of this book—misunderstandings in regard to the nature of what is here described as the aura. We might imagine that what are here described as colors would stand before the soul just as the physical colors stand before the physical eye, but such a soul color would be nothing but hallucination. Spiritual science is not in the least concerned with hallucinatory impressions, and they are, in any case, not what is meant in the description now before us. We reach a correct conception if we keep the following in mind. With a physical color, the soul experiences not only the sense impression, but through it, it has a soul-experience. When through the eye the soul perceives a yellow surface, this soul-experience is different from what it is when it perceives a blue surface. One may call this experience "living in yellow" or "living in blue." Now the soul that has followed the path of knowledge has a similar "experience in yellow" when observing the active soul-experience of other beings; an "experience in blue" when observing devotional soul-moods. The essential thing is not that the

143

seer in a visualization of another soul sees blue just as he sees this blue in the physical world, but that he has an experience that justifies his calling the visualization blue, just as the physical man calls a curtain blue, for instance. Further, it is essential that the seer should be conscious of standing in an experience free of the body so that he gains the possibility of speaking about the value and the meaning of the soul-life in a world whose perception is not mediated through the human body. Although this meaning of the description must be taken into account, yet it is altogether a matter of course for the seer to speak of blue, yellow, green, and so forth, in the aura. The aura varies greatly according to the different temperaments and dispositions of people. It likewise varies in accordance with the stages of spiritual development. A man who yields completely to his animal impulses has an entirely different aura from one who lives much in the world of thought. The aura of a religiously disposed nature differs essentially from one that loses itself in the trivial experiences of the day. In addition to this, all varying moods, all inclinations, joys and pains, find their expression in the aura.

We have to compare the auras of various soul-experiences with each other in order to learn to understand the meaning of the color shades. To begin with, take soul-experiences shot through with strongly marked emotions. They may be divided into two kinds—those in which the soul is impelled to these emotions chiefly by the animal nature, and those in which these passions take a

144

more subtle form, in which they are, so to speak, strongly influenced by reflection. In the first kind of experiences brown and reddish-yellow streams of color surge through the aura in definite locations. In persons with more subtle passions there appear in the same locations brighter reddish-yellow and green shades. One can notice that as intelligence increases the green shades become more frequent. Persons who are very intelligent, but who give themselves over entirely to satisfying their animal impulses, show much green in their aura, but this green will always have an admixture more or less of brown or brownish-red. Unintelligent people show a great part of their aura permeated by brownish-red or even by dark blood-red currents.

The auras of quiet, meditative, thoughtful soul-moods are essentially different from those of such passionate conditions. The brownish and reddish tones become less prominent and various shades of green emerge. In strenuous thinking the aura shows a pleasing green undertone. This is to a special degree the appearance of those natures who know how to adapt themselves to every condition of life.

Shades of blue appear in soul-moods full of devotion. The more a man places his self in the service of a cause, the more pronounced become the blue shades. In this class also one finds two quite different kinds of people. There are natures who are not in the habit of exerting their power of thought—passive souls who, as it were,

145

have nothing to throw into the streams of events in the world but their good nature. Their aura glimmers with a beautiful blue. This is also the appearance of many religious and devotional natures. Compassionate souls and those who find pleasure in giving themselves up to a life of benevolence have a similar aura. If such people are intelligent in addition, green and blue currents alternate, or the blue itself perhaps takes on a greenish shade. It is the peculiarity of the active souls in contrast to the passive, that their blue saturates itself from within with bright shades of color. Inventive natures, having fruitful thoughts, radiate bright shades of color as if from an inner center. This is true to the highest degree in those persons whom we call wise, and especially in those full of fruitful ideas. Generally speaking, all that implies spiritual activity takes more the form of rays spreading out from within, while everything that arises from the animal nature has the form of irregular clouds surging through the aura.

The variations in color nuances showing themselves in the corresponding aura formations depend on whether thoughts, springing from the soul's activity, are at the service of the soul's animal nature or that of an ideal, objective interest. The inventive person who applies all his thoughts to the satisfaction of his sensual passions shows dark blue-red shades. He, on the contrary, who places his thoughts selflessly at the service of an interest outside himself shows light reddish-blue color tones. A spiritual life

146

combined with noble devotion and capacity for sacrifice shows rose-pink or light violet colors.

Not only does the fundamental disposition of the soul show its color surgings in the aura, but also transient passions, moods and other inner experiences. A violent anger that breaks out suddenly creates red streams; feelings of injured dignity that expend themselves in a sudden welling up can be seen appearing in dark green clouds. Color phenomena, however, do not appear only in irregular cloud forms but also in distinctly defined, regularly shaped figures. If we observe a man under the influence of an attack of fear, we see this, for instance, in his aura from top to bottom as undulating stripes of blue color suffused with a bluish-red shimmer. When we observe a person who expects some particular event with anxiety, we can see red-blue stripes like rays constantly streaming through his aura from within outwards.

Every sensation received from without can be observed by the one who has developed the faculty of exact spiritual perception. Persons who are greatly excited by every external impression show a continuous flickering of small bluish-red spots and flecks in the aura. In people who do not feel intensely, these flecks have an orange-yellow or even a beautiful yellow coloring. So-called absent-mindedness shows bluish flecks playing over into green and more or less changing in form.

By means of a more highly developed spiritual vision

147

three species of color phenomena can be distinguished within the aura radiating and surging round a person. Firstly, there are colors that bear more or less the character of opaqueness and dullness. Certainly, if we compare them with colors seen with our physical eyes, they appear fugitive and transparent in comparison. Within the supersensible world itself, however, they make the space that they fill, comparatively speaking, opaque. They fill it in the manner of mist formations. A second species of colors consists of those that are light itself, as it were. They light up the space they fill so that it becomes through them itself a space of light. Color phenomena of the third kind are quite different from the first two. They have a raying, sparkling, glittering character. They fill space not merely with light but with glistening, glittering rays. There is something active and inherently mobile in these colors. The others are somewhat quiet and lack brilliance. These, on the contrary, continuously produce themselves out of themselves, as it were. Space is filled by the first two species of colors with a subtle fluidity that remains quietly in it. By the third, space is filled with an ever self-enkindling life, with never resting activity.

These three species of colors, however, are not ranged alongside each other in the human aura. They are not each enclosed in a separate section of space, but they interpenetrate and suffuse each other in the most varied ways. All three species can be seen playing through each other in one region of the aura, just as a physical body,

148

such as a bell, can simultaneously be heard and seen. The aura thus becomes an exceedingly complicated phenomenon because we have to do with three auras within each other, interpenetrating each other. We can, however, overcome the difficulty by directing our attention to the three species alternately. In the supersensible world we then do something similar to what we do in the sensible, for example, when we close our eyes in order to give ourselves up fully to the impressions of a piece of music. The seer has three different organs for the three species of color, and in order to observe undisturbed, he can open or close any one of the organs to impressions. As a rule only one kind of organ can at first be developed by a seer, namely, the organ for the first species of color. A person at this stage can see only the one aura; the other two remain invisible to him. In the same way a person may be accessible to impressions from the first two but not from the third. The higher stage of the gift of seeing consists in a person's being able to see all three auras, and for the purpose of study to direct his attention to the one or the other.

The threefold aura is thus the supersensibly visible expression of the being of man. The three members, body, soul and spirit, come to expression in it.

The first aura is a mirror of the influence the body exercises on the human soul; the second characterizes the life of the soul itself, the soul that has raised itself above the direct influence of the senses, but is not yet devoted to the service of the eternal; the third mirrors the mastery the eternal spirit has won over the transitory man. When descriptions of the aura are given, as here, it must be emphasized that these things are not only difficult to observe but above all difficult to describe. No one, therefore, should see in a description like this anything more than a stimulus to thought.

Thus, for the seer, the peculiarity of the soul's life expresses itself in the constitution of the aura. When he encounters a soul life that is given up entirely to passing impulses, passions and momentary external incitements, he sees the first aura in loudest colors; the second, on the contrary is only slightly developed. He sees in it only scanty color formations, while the third is barely indicated. Only here and there a small glittering spark of color shows itself, indicating that even in such a soul-mood the eternal already lives in man as a germ, but that it is driven into the background by the action of the sensory nature as has been indicated. The more a man gets rid of his lower impulses, the less obtrusive becomes the first part of the aura. The second part then grows larger and larger, filling the color body within which the physical man lives ever more completely with its illuminating force. The more a man proves himself to be a servant of the eternal, the more does the wonderful third aura show itself to be the part that bears witness to the extent to which he has become a citizen of the spiritual world because the divine self radiates into the earthly world

150

through this part of the human aura. Insofar as men show this aura, they are flames through whom the Godhead illumines this world. They show through this part of the aura how far they know how to live not for themselves, but for the eternally True, the nobly Beautiful and the Good. They show how far they have wrung from their narrower self the power to offer themselves up on the altar of cosmic world activity.

Thus there comes to expression in the aura what a man has made of himself in the course of his incarnations.

All three parts of the aura contain colors of the most varied shades, but the character of these shades changes with the stage of a man's development. In the first part of the aura there can be seen the undeveloped life of impulse in all shades from red to blue. These shades have a dull, muddy character. The obtrusive red shades point to the sensual desires, to the fleshly lusts, to the passion for the enjoyments of the palate and the stomach. Green shades appear to be found especially in those lower natures that incline to obtuseness and indifference, greedily giving themselves over to each enjoyment, but nevertheless shunning the exertions necessary to bring them to satisfaction. Where the desires are passionately bent on some goal beyond the reach of the capacities already acquired, brownish-green and yellowish-green auric colors appear. Certain modern modes of life actually breed this kind of aura.

A personal conceit that is entirely rooted in low inclinations, thus representing the lowest stage of egotism, shows

151

itself in tones of muddy yellow to brown. Now it is clear that the animal life of impulse can take on a pleasing character. There is a purely natural capacity for self-sacrifice, a high form of which is to be found even in the animal kingdom. This development of an animal impulse finds its most beautiful consummation in natural mother love. These selfless natural impulses come to expression in the first aura in light reddish to rose-red shades of color. Cowardly fear and timidity in the face of external causes show themselves in the aura in brown-blue and grey-blue colors.

The second aura again shows the most varied grades of colors. Brown and orange colored formations point to strongly developed conceit, pride and ambition. Inquisitiveness also announces its presence through red-yellow flecks. A bright yellow mirrors clear thinking and intelligence; green expresses understanding of life and the world. Children who learn easily have much green in this part of the aura. A green yellow in the second aura seems to betoken a good memory. Rose-red indicates a benevolent, affectionate nature; blue is the sign of piety. The more piety approaches religious fervor, the more does the blue pass over into violet. Idealism and an earnest view of life in a higher sense is to be seen as indigo blue.

The fundamental colors of the third aura are yellow, green and blue. Bright yellow appears here if the thinking is filled with lofty, comprehensive ideas that grasp the details as part of the whole of the divine world order. If the thinking is intuitive and also completely purified of all sensuous visualizations, the yellow has a golden brilliance. Green expresses love towards all beings; blue is the sign of a capacity for selfless sacrifice for all beings. If this capacity for sacrifice rises to the height of strong willing, devoting itself to the active service of the world, the blue brightens to light violet. If pride and desire for honor, as last remnants of personal egoism, are still present despite a more highly developed soul nature, others verging on orange appear beside the yellow shades. It must be remarked, however, that in this part of the aura the colors are quite different from the shades we are accustomed to see in the world of the senses. The seer beholds a beauty and an exaltedness with which nothing in the ordinary world can be compared.

This presentation of the aura cannot be rightly judged by anyone who does not attach the chief weight to the fact that the seeing of the aura implies an extension and enrichment of what is perceived in the physical world—an extension, indeed, that aims at knowing the form of the soul life that possesses spiritual reality apart from the world of the senses. This whole presentation has nothing whatever to do with reading character or a man's thoughts from an aura perceived in the manner of a hallucination. It seeks to expand knowledge in the direction of the spiritual world and has nothing in common with the questionable art of reading human souls from their auras.

CHAPTER IV

THE PATH OF KNOWLEDGE

K NOWLEDGE of the spiritual science that is aimed at in this book can be acquired by every man for himself. Descriptions of the kind given here present a thought picture of the higher worlds, and they are in a certain respect the first step towards personal vision. Man is a thought being, and *he can find his path to knowledge only when he makes thinking his starting-point.* A picture of the higher worlds given to his intellect is not without value for him even if for the time being it is only like a story about higher facts into which he has not yet gained insight through his own perception. The thoughts that are given him represent in themselves a force that continues working in his thought world. This force will be active in him; it will awaken slumbering capacities. Whoever is of the opinion that it is superfluous to give himself up to such a thought picture is mistaken because he regards thought as something unreal and abstract. Thought is a living force, and just as for one who has knowledge, thought is present

154

as a direct expression of what is seen in the spirit, so the imparting of this expression acts in the one to whom it is communicated as a germ that brings forth from itself the fruit of knowledge.

Anyone disdaining the application of strenuous mental exertion in the effort to attain the higher knowledge, and preferring to make use of other forces in man to that end, fails to take into account the fact that thinking is the highest of the faculties possessed by man in the world of the senses.

To him who asks, "How can I gain personal knowledge of the higher truths of spiritual science?" the answer must be given, "Begin by making yourself acquainted with what is communicated by others concerning such knowledge." Should he reply, "I wish to see for myself; I do not wish to know anything about what others have seen," one must answer, "It is in the very assimilating of the communications of others that the first step towards personal knowledge consists." If he then should answer, "Then I am forced to have blind faith to begin with," one can only reply, "In regard to something communicated it is not a case of belief or unbelief, but merely of an unprejudiced assimilation of what one hears." The true spiritual researcher never speaks with the expectation of meeting blind faith in what he says. He merely says, "I have experienced this in the spiritual regions of existence and I narrate my experiences." He knows also that the reception of

155

these experiences by another and the permeation of his thoughts with such an account are living forces making for spiritual development.

What is here to be considered will only be rightly viewed by one who takes into account the fact that all knowledge of the worlds of soul and spirit slumbers in the profoundest depths of the human soul. It can be brought to light through the path of knowledge. We can grasp, however, not only what we have ourselves brought to light, but also what someone else has brought up from those depths of the soul. This is so even when we have ourselves not yet made any preparations for the treading of that path of knowledge. Correct spiritual insight awakens the power of comprehension in anyone whose inner nature is not beclouded by preconceptions and prejudices. Unconscious knowledge flashes up to meet the spiritual fact discovered by another, and this "flashing up" is not blind faith but the right working of healthy human understanding. In this same healthy comprehension we should see a far better starting-point even for first hand cognition of the spiritual world than in dubious mystical contemplations or anything of a similar nature, in which we often fancy that we have something better than what is recognized by the healthy human understanding, when the results of genuine spiritual research are brought before it.

One cannot, in fact, emphasize strongly enough how necessary it is that anyone who wishes to develop his ca-

156

pacity for higher knowledge should undertake the earnest cultivation of his powers of thought. This emphasis must be all the more pressing because many persons who wish to become seers actually estimate lightly this earnest, self-denying labor of thinking. They say, "Thinking cannot help me to reach anything; the chief thing is sensation or feeling." In reply it must be said that no one can in the higher sense, and that means in truth, become a seer who has not previously worked himself into the life of thought. In this connection a certain inner laziness plays an injurious role with many persons. They do not become conscious of this laziness because it clothes itself in a contempt of abstract thought and idle speculation. We completely misunderstand what thinking is, however, if we confuse it with a spinning of idle, abstract trains of thought. Just as this abstract thinking can easily kill supersensible knowledge, so vigorous thinking, full of life, must be the groundwork on which it is based.

It would, indeed, be more comfortable if one could reach the higher power of seeing while shunning the labor of thinking. Many would like this, but in order to reach it an inner firmness is necessary, an assurance of soul to which thinking alone can lead. Otherwise there results merely a meaningless flickering of pictures here and there, a distracting display of soul phenomena that indeed gives pleasure to many, but that has nothing to do with a true penetration into the higher worlds. Further, if we consider

157

what purely spiritual experiences take place in a man who really enters the higher world, we shall then understand that the matter has still another aspect. Absolute healthiness of the soul life is essential to the condition of being a seer. There is no better means of developing this healthiness than genuine thinking. In fact, it is possible for this healthiness to suffer seriously if the exercises for higher development are not based on thinking. Although it is true that the power of spiritual sight makes a healthy and correctly thinking man still healthier and more capable in life than he is without it, it is equally true that all attempts to develop oneself while shirking the effort of thought, all vague dreamings in this domain, lend strength to fantasy and illusion and tend to place the seeker in a false attitude towards life. No one who wishes to develop himself to higher knowledge has anything to fear if he pays heed to what is said here, but the attempt should only be made under the above pre-supposition. This pre-supposition has to do only with man's soul and spirit. To speak of any conceivable kind of injurious influence upon the bodily health is absurd under this assumption.

Unfounded disbelief is indeed injurious. It works in the recipient as a repelling force. It hinders him from receiving fructifying thoughts. Not blind faith, but just this reception of the thought world of spiritual science is the prerequisite to the development of the higher senses. The spiritual researcher approaches his student with the injunction, "You are not required to believe what I tell you but to think it, to make it the content of your own thought world, then my thoughts will of themselves bring about your recognition of their truth." This is the attitude of the spiritual researcher. He gives the stimulus. The power to accept what is said as true springs forth from the inner being of the learner himself. It is in this manner that the views of spiritual science should be studied. Anyone who has the self-control to steep his thoughts in them may be sure that after a shorter or longer period of time they will lead him to personal perception.

In what has been said here, there is already indicated one of the first qualities that everyone wishing to acquire a vision of higher facts has to develop. It is the unreserved, unprejudiced laying of oneself open to what is revealed by human life or by the world external to man. If a man approaches a fact in the world around him with a judgment arising from his life up to the present, he shuts himself off by this judgment from the quiet, complete effect that the fact can have on him. The learner must be able each moment to make of himself a perfectly empty vessel into which the new world flows. Knowledge is received only in those moments in which every judgment, every criticism coming from ourselves, is silent. For example, when we meet a person, the question is not at all whether we are wiser than he. Even the most unreasoning child has something to reveal to the greatest sage. If he approaches the

159

child with his prejudgment, be it ever so wise, he pushes his wisdom like a dulled glass in front of what the child ought to reveal to him.*

Complete inner selflessness is necessary for this yielding of oneself up to the revelations of the new world. If a man tests himself to find out in what degree he possesses this accessibility to its revelations, he will make astonishing discoveries regarding himself. Anyone who wishes to tread the path of higher knowledge must train himself to be able at any given moment to obliterate himself with all his prejudices. As long as he obliterates himself the revelations of the new world flow into him. Only a high grade of such selfless surrender enables a man to receive the higher spiritual facts that surround him on all sides. We can consciously develop this capacity in ourselves. We can try, for example, to refrain from any judgment on people around us. We should obliterate within ourselves the gauge of "attractive" and "repellent," of "stupid" or "clever," that we are accustomed to apply and try without this gauge to understand persons purely from and through themselves. The best exercises can be made with people for whom one has an aversion. We should suppress this aversion with all our power and allow everything that they do to affect us without bias. Or, if we are in an environ-

* One can very well see, precisely from what is stated here, that in the requirement of "unreservedly laying onself open" there is no question of shutting out one's own judgment or of giving oneself up to blind faith. Anything of that sort would quite obviously have no sense or meaning in regard to a child.

ment that calls forth this or that judgment, we should suppress the judgment, and, free from criticism, lay ourselves open to impressions.*

We should allow things and events to speak to us rather than speak about them ourselves, and we also should extend this to our thought world. We should suppress in ourselves what prompts this or that thought and allow only what is outside to produce the thoughts. Only when such exercises are carried out with holiest earnestness and perseverance do they lead to the goal of higher knowledge. He who undervalues such exercises knows nothing of their worth, and he who has experience in such things knows that selfless surrender and freedom from prejudice are true producers of power. Just as heat applied to the steam boiler is transformed into the motive power of the locomotive, so do these exercises in selfless, spiritual self-surrender transform themselves in man into the power of seeing in the spiritual worlds.

By this exercise a man makes himself receptive to all that surrounds him, but to this receptivity he must allow correct valuation also to be added. As long as he is inclined to value himself too highly at the expense of the world around him, he bars himself from the approach to higher knowledge. The seeker who yields himself up to

---

* This open-minded and uncritical laying of ourselves open has nothing whatever to do with blind faith. The important thing is not that we should believe blindly in anything, but that we should not put a blind judgment in the place of the living impression.

the pleasure or pain that any thing or event in the world causes him is enmeshed by such an overvaluation of himself. Through *his* pleasure and *his* pain he learns nothing about the things, but merely something about himself. If I feel sympathy with a man, I feel to begin with nothing but *my* relation to him. If I make myself mainly dependent on this feeling of pleasure, of sympathy, for my judgment and my conduct, I place my personality in the foreground—I obtrude it upon the world. I want to thrust myself into the world just as I am, instead of accepting the world in an unbiased way, allowing it to assert itself in accordance with the forces acting in it. In other words I am tolerant only of what harmonizes with my peculiarities. In regard to everything else I exert a repelling force. As long as a man is enmeshed by the sensible world, he acts in an especially repelling way on all influences that are non-sensory. The learner must develop in himself the capacity to conduct himself toward things and people in accordance with their own peculiar natures, and to allow each of them to count at its due worth and significance. Sympathy and antipathy, pleasure and displeasure, must be made to play quite new roles. It is not a question here of man's eradicating them, of his blunting himself to sympathy and antipathy. On the contrary, the more a man develops the capacity to refrain from allowing each feeling of sympathy and antipathy to be followed immediately by a judgment, an action, the finer will his sensitivity become. He will find that sympathies and antipathies take on a higher char-

162

acter if he curbs those he already has. Even something that is at first most unattractive has hidden qualities. It reveals them if a man does not in his conduct obey his selfish feelings. A person who has developed himself in this respect has in every way a greater delicacy of feeling than one who is undeveloped because he does not allow his own personality to make him unimpressionable. Every inclination that a man follows blindly blunts the power to see things in his environment in their true light. By obeying inclination we thrust ourselves through the environment instead of laying ourselves open to it and feeling its true worth.

Man becomes independent of the changing impressions of the outer world when each pleasure and pain, each sympathy and antipathy, no longer call forth in him an egotistical response and conduct. The pleasure we feel in a thing makes us at once dependent on it. We lose ourselves in it. A man who loses himself in the pleasure or pain caused by every varying impression cannot tread the path of spiritual knowledge. He must accept pleasure and pain with equanimity. Then he ceases to lose himself in them and he begins instead to understand them. A pleasure to which I surrender myself devours my being in the moment of surrender. I should use the pleasure only in order to arrive through it at an understanding of the thing that arouses pleasure in me. The important point should not be that the thing has aroused pleasure in me. I should experience the pleasure and through it the nature of the

163

thing. The pleasure should only be an intimation to me that there is in the thing a quality capable of giving pleasure. This quality I must learn to understand. If I go no farther than the pleasure, if I allow myself to be entirely absorbed in it, then it is only myself who lives in it. If the pleasure is only the opportunity for me to experience a quality or property of the thing itself, I enrich my inner being through this experience. To the seeker, pleasure and displeasure, joy and pain, must be opportunities for learning about things. The seeker does not become blunted to pleasure or pain through this. He raises himself above them in order that they may reveal to him the nature of the things. By developing himself in this respect, he will learn to understand what instructors pleasure and pain are. He will feel with every being and thereby receive the revelation of its inner nature. The seeker never says to himself merely, "Oh, how I suffer!" or "Oh, how glad I am!" but always, "How does suffering speak? How does joy speak?" He eliminates the element of self in order that pleasure and joy from the outer world may work on him. By this means there develops in a man a completely new manner of relating himself to things. Formerly he responded to this or that impression by this or that action, only because the impressions caused him joy or unhappiness. Now he causes pleasure and displeasure to become also the organs by which things tell him what they themselves really are in their own nature. Pleasure and pain change from mere feelings within him to organs of sense by which the external world is perceived. Just as the eye does not act itself when it sees something, but causes the hand to act, so pleasure and pain do not bring about anything in the spiritual seeker insofar as he employs them as means of knowledge, but they receive impressions, and what is experienced through pleasure and displeasure causes the action. When a man uses pleasure and displeasure in such a way that they become organs of transmission, they build up for him within his soul the actual organs through which the soul world opens up to view. The eye can serve the body only by being an organ for the transmission of sense impressions. Pleasure and pain become the *eyes of the soul* when they cease to be of value merely to themselves and begin to reveal to one's soul the other soul outside it.

By means of the qualities mentioned, the seeker for knowledge places himself in a condition that allows what is really present in the world around him to act upon him without disturbing influences from his own peculiarities. He has also to fit himself into the spiritual world around him in the right way because he is as a thinking being a citizen of the spiritual world. He can be this in the right way only if during mental activity he makes his thoughts run in accordance with the eternal laws of truth, the laws of the spiritland. Only thus can that land act on him and reveal its facts to him. A man never reaches the truth as long as he gives himself up to the thoughts continually coursing through his ego. If he permits this, his thoughts

165

take a course imposed on them by the fact of their coming into existence within the bodily nature. The thought world of a man who gives himself up to a mental activity determined primarily by his physical brain looks irregular and confused. In it a thought enters, breaks off, is driven out of the field by another. Anyone who tests this by listening to a conversation between two people, or who observes himself in an unprejudiced way, will gain an idea of this mass of confused thoughts. As long as a man devotes himself only to the calls of the life of the senses, his confused succession of thoughts will always be set right again by the facts of reality. I may think ever so confusedly but in my actions everyday facts force upon me the laws corresponding to the reality. My mental picture of a city may be most confused, but if I wish to walk along a certain road in the city, I must accommodate myself to the conditions it imposes on me. The mechanic can enter his workshop with ever so varied a whirl of ideas, but the laws of his machines compel him to adopt the correct procedure in his work. Within the world of the senses facts exercise their continuous corrective on thought. If I come to a false opinion by thinking about a physical phenomenon or the shape of a plant, the reality confronts me and sets my thinking right.

It is quite different when I consider my relations to the higher regions of existence. They reveal themselves to me only if I enter their worlds with already strictly controlled thinking. There my thinking must give me the right, the

166

he has recognized as right and find his personal feelings not satisfied by that action, he must not for that reason forsake the road he has entered on. On the other hand, he must not pursue it just because it gives him joy, if he finds that it is not in accordance with the laws of the eternally beautiful and true. In everyday life people allow their actions to be decided by what satisfies them personally, by what bears fruit for themselves. In so doing they force upon the world's events the direction of their personality. They do not bring to realization the true that is traced out in the laws of the spirit world, rather do they realize the demands of their self-will. We only act in harmony with the spiritual world when we follow its laws alone. From what is done only out of the personality, there result no forces that can form a basis for spiritual knowledge. The seeker of knowledge may not ask only, "What brings me advantages; what will bring me success?" He must also be able to ask, "What have I recognized as the good?" Renunciation of the fruits of action for his personality, renunciation of all self-will; these are the stern laws that he must prescribe for himself. Then he treads the path of the spiritual world, his whole being penetrated by these laws. He becomes free from all compulsion from the sense world; his spirit man raises itself out of the sensory sheath. He thus makes actual progress on the path towards the spiritual and thus he spiritualizes himself. One may not say, "Of what use to me are the resolutions to follow purely the laws of the true when I am perhaps mistaken concerning what is true?" The important thing is the striving, and the spirit in which one strives. Even when the seeker is mistaken, he possesses, in his very striving for the true, a force that turns him away from the wrong road. Should he be mistaken, this force seizes him and guides him to the right road. The very objection, "But I may be mistaken," is itself harmful unbelief. It shows that the man has no confidence in the power of the true. The important point is that he should not presume to decide on his aims in accordance with his own egotistical views, but that he should selflessly yield himself up to the guidance of the spirit itself. It is not the self-seeking will of man that can prescribe for the true. On the contrary, what is true must itself become lord in man, must permeate his whole being, make him a copy of the eternal laws of the spiritland. He must fill himself with these eternal laws in order to let them stream out into life.

Just as the seeker of knowledge must be able to have strict control of his thinking, so he must also have control of his will. Through this he becomes in all modesty—without presumption—a messenger of the world of the true and the beautiful. Through this he ascends to be a participant in the spirit world. Through this he is lifted from stage to stage of development because one cannot reach the spiritual life by merely seeing it. On the contrary, one has to reach it by experiencing it, by living it.

If the seeker of knowledge observes the laws here described, his soul experiences relating to the spiritual world will take on an entirely new form. He will no longer live merely within them. They will no longer have a significance merely for his personal life. They will develop into soul perceptions of the higher world. In his soul the feelings of pleasure and displeasure, of joy and pain, do not live for themselves only, but grow into soul organs, just as in his body eyes and ears do not lead a life for themselves alone but selflessly allow external impressions to pass through them. Thereby the seeker of knowledge wins that calmness and assurance in his soul constitution necessary for research in the spirit world. A great pleasure will no longer make him merely jubilant, but may be the messenger to him of qualities in the world that have hitherto escaped him. It will leave him calm, and through the calm the characteristics of the pleasure-giving beings will reveal themselves to him. Pain will no longer merely fill him with grief, but be able to tell him also what the qualities are of the being that causes the pain. Just as the eye does not desire anything for itself but shows man the direction of the road he has to take, so will pleasure and pain guide the soul safely along its path. This is the state of balance of soul that the seeker of knowledge must reach. The less pleasure and pain exhaust themselves in the waves that they throw up in the inner life of the seeker of knowledge, the more will they form eyes for the supersensible world. As long as a man lives in pleasure and pain he cannot gain knowledge by means of them. When he learns how to live by means of them, when he withdraws his feeling of self from them, then they become his organs of perception and he sees by means of them, attaining through them to knowledge. It is incorrect to think that the seeker of knowledge becomes a dry, colorless being, incapable of experiencing joy and sorrow. Joy and sorrow are present in him, but when he seeks knowledge in the spiritual world, they are present in a transformed shape; they have become eyes and ears.

As long as we live in a personal relationship with the world, things reveal only what links them with our personality. This, however, is their transitory part. If we withdraw ourselves from our transitory part and live with our feeling of self, with our "I," in our permanent part, then our transitory part becomes an intermediary for us. What reveals itself through it is an imperishable, an eternal in the things. The seeker of knowledge must be able to establish this relationship between his own eternal part and the eternal in the things. Even before he begins other exercises of the kind described, and also during them, he should direct his thought to this imperishable part. When I observe a stone, a plant, an animal or a man, I should be able to remember that in each of them an eternal expresses itself. I should be able to ask myself, "What is the permanent that lives in the transitory stone, in the transitory man? What will outlast the transitory sensory appearance?" We ought not to think that to direct the spirit to the eternal in this way destroys our careful consideration of, and sense for, the qualities of everyday affairs and estranges us from the immediate realities. On the contrary, every leaf, every little insect will unveil to us innumerable mysteries when not only our eyes but through the eyes the spirit is directed upon them. Every sparkle, every shade of color, every cadence will remain vividly perceptible to the senses. Nothing will be lost, but in addition, unlimited new life will be gained. Indeed, the person who does not understand how to observe even the tiniest thing with the eye, will only attain to pale, bloodless thoughts, not to spiritual sight.

It depends upon the attitude of mind we acquire in this direction. What stage we shall succeed in reaching will depend on our capacities. We have only to do what is right and leave everything else to evolution. It must be enough for us at first to direct our minds to the permanent. If we do this, the knowledge of the permanent will awaken in us through this. We must wait until it is given, and it is given at the right time to each one who with patience waits and *works*. A man soon notices during such exercises what a mighty transformation takes place within him. He learns to consider each thing as important or unimportant only insofar as he recognizes it to be related to a permanent, to an eternal. He comes to a valuation and estimate of the world different from the one he has hitherto had. His whole feeling takes on a new relationship toward the entire surrounding world. The transitory no longer attracts him merely for its own sake as formerly. It becomes for him a member, an image of the eternal, and this eternal, living in all things, he learns to love. It becomes familiar, just as the transitory was formerly familiar to him. This again does not cause his estrangement from life. He only learns to value each thing according to its true significance. Even the vain trifles of life will not pass him by quite without trace, but the man seeking after the spiritual no longer loses himself in them, but recognizes them at their limited worth. He sees them in their true light. He is a poor discerner of the spiritual who would go wandering in the clouds losing sight of life. From his high summit a true discerner with his power of clear survey and his just and healthy feeling for everything will know how to assign to each thing its proper place.

Thus there opens out to the seeker of knowledge the possibility of ceasing to obey only the unreliable influences of the external world of the senses that turn his will now here, now there. Through higher knowledge he has seen the eternal being of things. By means of the transformations of his inner world he has gained the capacity for perceiving this eternal being. For the seeker of knowledge the following thoughts have a special weight. When he acts out of himself, he is then conscious of acting also out of the eternal being of things because the things give utterance in him to their being. He, therefore, acts in harmony with the eternal world order when he directs his action out of the eternal living within him. He thus knows himself no longer merely as a being impelled by things. He knows that he impels them according to the laws

174

implanted within them that have become the laws of his own being. This ability to act out of his inner being can only be an ideal towards which he strives. The attainment of the goal lies in the far distance, but the seeker of knowledge must have the will to recognize clearly this road. This is his will to freedom, for freedom is action out of one's inner being. Only he may act out of his inner being who draws his motives from the eternal. A being who does not do this, acts according to other motives than those implanted in things. Such a person opposes the world order, and the world order must then prevail against him. That is to say, what he plans to carry through by his will cannot in the last resort take place. He cannot become free. The arbitrary will of the individual being annihilates itself through the effects of its deeds.

* * *

Whoever is able to work upon his inner life in such a way climbs upwards from stage to stage in spiritual knowledge. The reward of his exercises will be the unfolding of certain vistas of the supersensible world to his spiritual perception. He learns the real meaning of the truths communicated about this world, and he will receive confirmation of them through his own experience. If this stage is reached, he encounters an experience that can only come through treading this path. Something occurs whose significance can only now become clear to him.

175

Through the great spiritual guiding powers of the human race there is bestowed on him what is called initiation. He becomes a disciple of wisdom. The less one sees in such initiation something that consists in an outer human relationship, the more correct will be his conception of it. What the seeker of knowledge now experiences can only be indicated here. He receives a new home. He becomes thereby a conscious dweller in the supersensible world. The source of spiritual insight now flows to him from a higher region. The light of knowledge from this time forth does not shine upon him from without, but he is himself placed at its fountainhead where the problems that the world offers receive a new illumination. Henceforth he holds converse no longer with the things that are shaped by the spirit, but with the shaping spirit itself. At the moments of attaining spiritual knowledge, the personality's own life exists now only in order to be a conscious image of the eternal. Doubts about the spirit that could formerly arise in him vanish because only he can doubt who is deluded by things regarding the spirit ruling in them. Since the disciple of wisdom is able to hold intercourse with the spirit itself, each false form vanishes in which he had previously imagined the spirit. The false form under which one conceives the spirit is superstition. the initiate has passed beyond all superstition because he has knowledge of the spirit's true form. Freedom from the prejudices of the personality, of doubt, and of supersition—these are the characteristics of the seeker who has attained to discipleship on the path of higher knowledge. We must not confuse this state in which the personality becomes one with the all-embracing spirit of life, with an absorption into the universal spirit that annihilates the personality. Such a disappearance does not take place in a true development of the personality. Personality continues to be preserved as such in the relationship into which it enters with the spirit world. It is not the subjection of the personality, but its highest development that occurs. If we wish to have a simile for this coincidence or union of the individual spirit with the all-encompassing spirit, we cannot choose that of many different coinciding circles that are lost in one circle, but we must choose the picture of many circles, each of which has a quite distinct shade of color. These variously colored circles coincide, but each separate shade preserves its color existence within the whole. Not one loses the fulness of its individual power.

The further description of the path will not be given here. It is given as far as possible in my *Occult Science, an Outline,* which forms a continuation of this book.

What is said here about the path of spiritual knowledge can all too easily, through failure to understand it, tempt us to consider it as a recommendation to cultivate certain moods of soul that would lead us to turn away from the immediate, joyous and strenuously active, experience of life. As against this, it must be emphasized that the particular attitude of the soul that renders it fit to experience

177

directly the reality of the spirit, cannot be extended as a general demand over the entire life. It is possible for the seeker after spiritual existence to bring his soul for the purpose of research into the necessary condition of being withdrawn from the realities of the senses, without that withdrawal estranging him from the world. On the other hand, however, it must be recognized that a knowledge of the spiritual world, not merely a knowledge gained by treading the path, but also a knowledge acquired through grasping the truths of spiritual science with the unprejudiced, healthy human intellect, leads also to a higher moral status in life, to a knowledge of sensory existence that is in accord with the truth, to certainty in life, and to inward health of the soul.

ADDENDA

ADDENDA

No. 1. To speak of a vital force was still regarded a short time ago as a sign of an unscientific mind. Today there are here and there among scientists some who are not averse to the once entertained idea of a vital force. But anyone who examines the course of modern scientific development will, nevertheless, perceive the more consistent logic of those who, in view of this development, refuse to listen to anything about such a vital force. Certainly, vital force does not belong to what are called today forces of nature. Anyone who is not willing to pass from the habits of thought and the conceptions of modern science to a higher mode of thinking should not speak of vital force. Only the mode of thinking and the presuppositions of spiritual science make it possible to deal with such things without inconsistency. Further, those thinkers who seek to form their conclusions purely on the ground of modern science have abandoned the belief that obtained in the latter half of the nineteenth century, namely, that the phenomena of life could only be explained through references to the same forces that are at work in inanimate nature. The book of such a noted naturalist as Oskar Hertwig, *The Development of Organisms;*

181

A Refutation of Darwin's Theory of Chance, is a scientific phenomenon that sheds its light far and wide. It opposes the assumption that the inter-workings of mere physical and chemical laws are able to shape the living thing. It is also significant that, in so-called Neo-Vitalism, a view is becoming prevalent that also admits the activity of a special force in living things much after the manner of the older theory of vital force. In this domain, however, we shall never be able to get beyond shadowy abstract concepts unless we recognize that the only possible way of reaching what in life transcends in its activity the inorganic forces is by means of a mode of perception that rises to supersensible vision. The point is that the kind of knowledge modern science has been applying to the inorganic cannot be carried over into the region of life, but that an entirely different kind of knowledge must be acquired.

No. 2. When the sense of touch of the lower organisms is mentioned here, the word "sense" does not mean the same thing referred to by this term in the usual descriptions of the senses. Indeed, from the point of view of spiritual science, much can be said against the use of this word. What is meant here by sense of touch is rather the general attaining to awareness of an external impression in contrast to the special attaining to awareness that consists in seeing, hearing, and so forth.

182

No. 3. It may appear as if the manner of dividing the being of man employed in this book rests upon a purely arbitrary differentiation of parts within the unitary soul life. It must be emphasized that this differentiation within the unitary soul life may be compared with the phenomenon of the seven color nuances in the rainbow, caused by light passing through a prism. What the physicist accomplishes with his explanation of the phenomenon of light through his study of this process, and the resultant seven shades of color, is accomplished by the spiritual scientist with regard to the soul being of man. The seven members of the soul are not merely abstract distinctions of the intellect any more than are the seven colors in light. The differentiation rests in both cases upon the inner nature of the facts, except that the seven members in light become visible through an external contrivance, while the seven members of the soul become observable by a method consistent with the spiritual nature of the soul being of man. The soul's true nature cannot be grasped without the knowledge of this inner organization because the soul, through its three members, physical body, life body and soul body, belongs to the transitory world; through its other four members, it is rooted in the eternal. In the unitary soul the transitory and the eternal are indistinguishably united. Unless one is aware of this differentiation of the soul, it is not possible to understand its relation to the world as a whole. Another comparison

183

may also be used. The chemist separates water into hydrogen and oxygen. Neither of these substances can be observed in the unitary water. Nevertheless, each has its own proper existence. Hydrogen and oxygen both unite with other substances. Thus at death, the three lower members of the soul unite with the transitory part of the world being; the four higher members unite with the eternal. Anyone who objects to taking this differentiation of the soul into account resembles an analytical chemist who objects to knowing anything about the separation of water into hydrogen and oxygen.

No. 4. It is necessary that the statements of spiritual science be taken literally because only in the accurate expression of the ideas have they value. For example, take the sentence, "They (the sensations) do not, in its case (namely, that of the animal), become interwoven with independent thoughts, transcending the immediate experiences." If the words "independent, transcending the immediate experiences" are left out of account, it would be easy to fall into the mistake of thinking that it is claimed here that the sensations and instincts of animals do not contain thoughts. The truth is, that spiritual science is based on a knowledge that says that all inner experience of animals, as well as existence in general, is interwoven with thought. Only the thoughts of the animals are not those of an independent ego living in the animal, but those of the animal group-ego, which must be

184

regarded as a being governing the animal from without. This group-ego is not, like the human ego, present in the physical world, but works down into the animal from the soul world as described on page 70. (Further details regarding this are to be found in my *Occult Science, an Outline*.) The point to make clear is that in man, thought attains to an independent existence; that in him, it is not experienced indirectly in sensation, but directly in the soul as thought.

No. 5. When it is said that little children say, "Charles is good," "Mary wants to have this," it must be specially noted that the important point is not so much how soon children use the word "I," but when they connect the corresponding idea with that word. When children hear adults using the word, it is easy for them to use it too, without forming the idea of the "I." The generally late use of the word points to an important fact in evolution, namely, to the gradual unfolding of the idea "I" out of the dim "I" feeling.

No. 6. A description of the real nature of intuition is to be found in my books, *Knowledge of the Higher Worlds and Its Attainment,* and *Occult Science, an Outline.* Through lack of accurate attention, a contradiction might be detected between the use of the word in those two books, and what is said concerning it in this one (page 30). To the careful observer, however, this contradiction does not

185

exist. It will be seen that what is revealed in all its fulness from the spiritual world to supersensible perception, through intuition, makes itself known in its lowest manifestation in the spirit self, just as the external physical world makes itself known in sensation.

No. 7. On *Re-embodiment of the Spirit and Destiny.* Concerning the statements in this section of the book, it must be borne in mind that—disregarding for the moment the facts of spiritual science already given in other parts of the book—the attempt is made, by means of thoughtful observation of the course of human life, to gain an idea of the extent to which this human life with its destiny, points to repeated earth-lives. These ideas will, of course, appear questionable to those who regard the customary belief in a single life on earth as the only well-founded one. It should also be borne in mind, however, that the intention here is to show that the ordinary way of looking at things can never lead to an understanding of the deeper foundations of life. For this reason, other conceptions must be sought that apparently contradict the generally accepted ones. This search is only hindered by the deliberate refusal to apply the same thoughtful consideration to a course of events belonging to the soul, that is applied to a series of events in the physical world. In thus refusing, no value is attached, for instance, to the fact that when a stroke of fate falls upon the "I," the effect in the realm of feeling bears a relation to that produced when the memory meets an experience related to what is remembered. Anyone who tries to observe how a stroke of fate is really experienced will be able to differentiate between this experience and the assertions to which a point of view that is merely external must necessarily give rise, and through which, of course, every living connection between this stroke of fate and the ego is lost sight of. For such a point of view, the blow appears to be either the result of chance or to have been determined by some external cause. The fact that there are also strokes of fate that, in a certain way, break into a human life for the first time, only showing their results later on, makes the temptation all the greater to generalize on this basis without taking other possibilities into account.

People do not begin to pay heed to these other possibilities until experience of life has brought their imaginative faculty into a direction similar to the one that may be observed in Goethe's friend, Knebel, who wrote in a letter, "On close observation it will be seen that there is a plan in the lives of most people that seems traced out for them, either through their own nature or through the circumstances that affect them. The conditions of their lives may be ever so varied and changeable, but taken as a whole, a certain conformity will be apparent in the end. . . . However secretly it may operate, the hand of a definite destiny, whether moved by an outer cause or by an inner impulse, may be clearly discerned; even conflicting causes often move in its direction. However confused the course of life may be, plan and definite direction are always discernible."

It is easy to raise objections to observations of this kind, especially for people who are not willing to consider the experiences of the soul in which such observation has its origin. The author of this book, however, believes that in what he has said about repeated earth-lives and destiny, he has accurately drawn the boundary line within which one can form conceptions about the underlying causes shaping human life. He has pointed out the fact that the view to which these ideas lead can only be defined by them in silhouette-like form, that they can only prepare the thoughts for what must be discovered by means of spiritual science. This thought-preparation is an inner work of the soul. If it does not over-estimate itself, if it does not seek to prove, but aims merely at being an exercise of the soul, it makes a man impartially open to knowledge that must appear foolish, without such preparation.

No. 8. The subject of the spiritual organs of perception that is only alluded to briefly at the end of this book in the chapter on *The Path of Knowledge,* is more fully dealt with in my books, *Knowledge of the Higher Worlds and Its Attainment* and *Occult Science, an Outline.*

No. 9. It would be incorrect to imagine that there is ceaseless unrest in the spiritual world because "a state of rest, a remaining in one place such as we find in the physical world," does not exist there. It is true that where the "archetypes are creative beings," there is nothing that can be called "rest in one place," but there is the rest that is of a spiritual kind, and that is compatible with active mobility. It may be likened to the restful contentment and bliss of the spirit that is manifest in deeds, but not in being inactive.

No. 10. One is obliged to use the word "purposes" with regard to the great evolutionary powers of the world, although in so doing occasion is given to the temptation to conceive of these powers simply as one thinks of human purposes. In the case of such words, which have naturally to be taken from the sphere of the human world, this temptation can be avoided only by learning to perceive in them a new significance and meaning, from which all that they contain of the narrowly limited human element has been eliminated. In place of this a meaning may be imparted to them that is given to such words at those moments in life when a man rises to a certain extent above himself.

No. 11. Further particulars about the "Spiritual Word" are to be found in my *Occult Science, an Outline*.

No. 12. When it is said here, "Out of the Eternal he can determine the direction for the future," this is intended to point to the special way in which the human soul is constituted during the time between death and a new birth. A stroke of destiny that befalls a person during life in the physical world may seem, from the point of view of that (physical) life, to contain something altogether opposed to the man's own will. In the life between death and re-birth a force, resembling will, rules in the soul that gives to the person the tendency toward experiencing this very blow of fate. The soul sees, as it were, that an imperfection has clung to it from earlier earth-lives—an imperfection that had its origin in an ugly deed or an ugly thought. Between death and re-birth, there arises in the soul a will-like impulse to make good this imperfection. The soul, therefore, becomes imbued with the tendency to plunge into a misfortune in the coming earth-life, in order, through enduring it, to bring about equilibrium. After its birth in the physical body, the soul, when met by some hard fate, has no glimmering of the fact that in the purely spiritual life before birth, the impulse that led to this hard fate had been voluntarily accepted by it. What, therefore, seems completely unwished for from the point of view of the earth-life is willed by the soul itself in the supersensible. "Out of the Eternal man determines the future for himself."

No. 13. The section in this book on *Thought Forms and the Human Aura* is doubtless the one that may most easily lead to misconceptions. It is precisely with regard to these descriptions that antagonistic feelings find the best opportunity for raising objections. It is, indeed, natural to demand, for instance, that the statements of the seer in this domain should be proved by experiments corresponding to the scientific mode of thinking. It may be demanded that a number of people who assert that they are able to see the spiritual of the aura should place themselves in front of other people and allow their auras to work upon them. Then these seers should be asked to say what thoughts and feelings they see as the auras of the people they are observing. If their reports coincide, and if it is found that the persons observed really have had the feelings and thoughts reported by the seers, then one could believe in the existence of the aura. That is certainly thought quite scientifically. The following, however, must be taken into account. The work that the spiritual researcher does in his own soul, through which he acquires the capacity for spiritual vision, has, as its aim, the acquisition of this capacity. Whether he is then able in any given case to perceive something in the spiritual world does not depend upon himself, nor, for that matter, does what he perceives. That flows to him as a gift from the spiritual world. He cannot take it by force, but must wait until it comes to him. His intention to bring about the perception has no bearing on the real causes of its happening, but this intention is exactly what modern science demands for the experiment. The spiritual world, however, will not allow itself to be dictated to. If the above attempt is to succeed, it would have to be instituted from the spiritual world. In that world a being would have to have the intention of revealing the thoughts of one or more persons to one or more people who are able to "see." These seers would then have to be brought together through a spiritual impulse for their work of observation. In that case their reports would certainly coincide. Paradoxical as all this may appear to the purely scientific mind, it is, nevertheless, true.

Spiritual experiments cannot be undertaken in the same way as those of a physical nature. If the seer, for example, receives the visit of a person who is a stranger to him, he cannot at once undertake to observe the aura of this person, but he sees the aura when there is occasion in the spiritual world for it to be revealed to him. These few words are intended merely to draw attention to the misconception in the objection described above. What spiritual science has to do is to point the way by which a man may come to see the aura, by what means he may himself bring about the experiences of its reality. Thus the only reply that spiritual science can make to the would-be seer is, "The conditions have been made known; apply them to your own soul, and you will see." It would certainly be more convenient if the above demands of the modern scientific mode of thought could be fulfilled, but whoever asks for tests of this kind shows that he has not made himself acquainted with the very first results of spiritual science.

The statements made in this book about the human

192

aura are not intended to encourage the desire for super-sensible sensation. This desire only admits itself satisfied with regard to the spiritual world if it is shown something as "spirit" that cannot be distinguished in thought from the physically sensible, so that it can rest comfortably and remain with its conceptions in that same physical sense-world. What is said on page 143 about the way in which the auric color is to be imagined is certainly calculated to prevent such misunderstanding. Anyone, however, who is striving for true insight into these things must clearly perceive that the human soul, in experiencing the spiritual and psychic, has of necessity before it the spiritual, not the physical-sensible view of the aura. Without this view, the experience remains in the unconscious. It is a mistake to confuse the pictorial perception with the actual experience itself, but one ought also to make quite clear to oneself that in this same pictorial perception the experience finds a completely true expression; not one, for instance, that the beholding soul creates arbitrarily, but one that takes shape of itself in supersensible perception.

At the present time, a modern scientist would be forgiven should he feel called upon to speak of a kind of human aura such as Prof. Dr. Moritz Benedikt describes in his book on the *Rod and Pendulum Theory* (*Ruten und Pendellehre*). "There exist, even though in small numbers, human beings who are adapted to the dark. A relatively large fraction of this minority sees in the dark many objects without colors, and only relatively few see the

objects colored also. . . . A considerable number o
learned men and physicians have been subjected t
research in my dark room by my two classical 'subjects' o
'seers in the dark,' and those thus investigated could retai
no justifiable doubt as to the correctness of the observa
tions and descriptions . . . Now those persons 'adapted t
the dark' who see colors, see in the front the forehead and
scalp blue, and see the rest of the right half likewise blue
and the left red, or some see it . . . orange-yellow. To the
rear, the same division is found, and the same coloring."
The spiritual researcher is not so easily forgiven when he
speaks of the aura.

There is no intention here of taking up any kind of attitude toward all that Benedikt has worked out, which
belongs to the most interesting modern theories of nature
Neither is it intended to take advantage of a cheap op
portunity to make excuses for spiritual science through
natural science, which so many enjoy doing. It is only
intended to point out how, in one instance, a scientist car
be brought to make assertions that are not unlike those o
spiritual science. At the same time, it must be emphasized
that the aura that is spoken of in this book, and that car
only be grasped spiritually, is something quite different
from what can be investigated by physical means and
about which Benedikt speaks. We surrender ourselves to
a gross illusion if we think that the spiritual aura can be
one that may be subject to research by the external means
of modern science. That aura is only accessible to the

spiritual perception reached by the path of knowledge as described in the last chapter of this book. It would also be a mistake to suppose that the truth and reality of what is spiritually perceived can be demonstrated in the same way as can what is perceived through the senses.